Tunes on a Tin Whistle

SOME REAL-LIFE POETRY

Compiled by
ALAN CRANG

Wheaton
A Division of Pergamon Press

A. Wheaton & Company Limited
A Division of Pergamon Press
Hennock Road, Exeter EX2 8RP

Pergamon Press Ltd, Headington Hill Hall, Oxford OX3 0BW

Pergamon Press Inc., Maxwell House, Fairview Park, Elmsford,
New York 10523

Pergamon of Canada Ltd, Suite 104, 150 Consumers Road,
Willowdale, Ontario M2J 1P9

Pergamon Press (Australia) Pty Ltd, P.O. Box 544, Potts Point,
N.S.W. 2011

First edition 1967
Reprinted 1970, 1972, 1974, 1979, 1980
Library of Congress Catalog Card No. 67-21272

Printed in Great Britain by A. Wheaton & Co. Ltd, Exeter

ISBN 08 012478 X flexi net
ISBN 08 012480 8 flexi non net
ISBN 08 012479 8 hard net

For Janet, Benjamin and Nicolas

Contents

6. AGAINST THE LAW

7. CRABBED AGE AND YOUTH

8. LOVE'S ANOTHER THING

9. LIGHT YEARS APART

10.   LAUGHS AND AFTERTHOUGHTS

Acknowledgements

FOR permission to reprint copyright material the following acknowledgements are made:

W. H. Auden—"The Unknown Citizen"; "Roman Wall Blues" from *Collected Shorter Poems*; to the author and Messrs. Faber & Faber.

Leo Aylen—"If You'll Give Me a Kiss"; to the author.

Michael Baldwin—"Hunting with a Stick"; "The Housewife"; to Messrs. Routledge & Kegan Paul.

George Barker—"To My Mother" from *Collected Poems*; to the author and Messrs. Faber & Faber.

James Baxter—"A Rope for Harry Fat" from *Howrah Bridge and Other Poems*; to the author and Oxford University Press.

Patricia Beer—"The Fifth Sense" from *Loss of the Magyar and Other Poems*; to the author and Longmans, Green & Co. Ltd.

John Betjeman—"Hunter Trials" from *Collected Poems*; to John Murray Ltd.

A. C. Boyd—"Flute Player"; to the author.

Edwin Brock—"Song of a Battery Hen"; to The Scorpion Press.

Alan Brownjohn—"In This City"; to the author.

Jim Burns—"A Way of Looking at Things"; to the author.

Roy Campbell—"The Zulu Girl"; to Messrs. Curtis, Brown Ltd.

Charles Causley—"Death of an Aircraft"; "My Friend Maloney"; "Timothy Winters"; to Messrs. David Higham and Rupert Hart-Davis.

Austin Clarke—"Unmarried Mothers"; from *Poems* by Austin Clarke; to the author and Oxford University Press.

Tony Connor—"Bank Holiday"; "The Burglary"; "Elegy for Alfred Hubbard" from *With Love Somehow* and "Child's

Bouncing Song" from *The Lodgers*; to the author and Oxford University Press.

Alan Crang—"Sheep Gathering"; "South Wales Landscape"; to the author.

E. E. Cummings—"In just spring" from *Selected Poems*; to the author and Messrs. Faber & Faber.

Keith Douglas—"Vergissmeinicht"; to Mrs. Douglas and Messrs. Faber & Faber.

T. S. Eliot—"Preludes I and II" from *Collected Poems 1909–1962*; to the author and Messrs. Faber & Faber.

D. J. Enright—"The Poor Wake Up Quickly"; "The Proper Due" from *Some Men are Brothers*; to the author and Messrs. Chatto & Windus Ltd.

Lawrence Ferlinghetti—"Sometime During Eternity" from *A Coney Island of the Mind*; to the author and L. Pollinger Ltd.

Robert Frost—"Mending Wall"; "Out, Out" from *The Complete Poems of Robert Frost*; to the author and L. Pollinger Ltd., and Jonathan Cape.

Karen Gershon—"Race" from *Selected Poems*; to Victor Gollancz Ltd.

Zulfikar Ghose—"The President's Visit"; to Messrs. Routledge & Kegan Paul.

Robert Graves—"With Her Lips Only" from *Collected Poems, 1965*; to A. P. Watt & Son and International Author's N.V.

Thom Gunn—"Black Jackets" from *My Sad Captains*; "Elvis Presley" from *The Sense of Movement*; to the author and Messrs. Faber & Faber.

Thomas Hardy—"Channel Firing"; "In the Cemetery"; "The Man He Killed" from *The Collected Poems of Thomas Hardy*; to Macmillan & Co. Ltd., and the Trustees of Hardy Estate.

Seamus Heaney—"The Early Purges" from *Death of a Naturalist*; to the author and Messrs. Faber & Faber.

David Holbrook—"Cardoness Castle" from *Against The Cruel Frost*; "Fingers in the Door"; "Unholy Marriage" from *Imaginings*; to the author and Putnam and Co. Ltd.

G. M. Hopkins—"Felix Randal" from *Complete Poems of G. M. Hopkins*; to the author and Oxford University Press.

Michael Horovitz—"Blues for the Hitch-Hiking Dead"; to the author.

Ted Hughes—"Six Young Men"; "The Jaguar"; "Wind" from *Hawk in the Rain* and "View of a Pig" from *Lupercal*; to the author and Messrs. Faber & Faber.

Elizabeth Jennings—"Eighty-One Years Old"; "Father to Son"; "Old Man Asleep"; "The Young Ones"; "Woman With a Fatal Illness"; to Andre Deutsch Ltd.

B. S. Johnson—"Song of a Wagon Driver"; to Constable & Co. Ltd.

Philip Larkin—"Ambulances"; "The Whitsun Weddings" from *The Whitsun Weddings*; to the author and Messrs. Faber & Faber. "Poetry of Departures"; to the Marvell Press.

D. H. Lawrence—"Discord in Childhood"; "Let Us Be Men"; "The Effort of Love" from *The Complete Poems of D. H. Lawrence*; to L. Pollinger Ltd. and the estate of the late Mrs. Freida Lawrence.

Laurie Lee—"The Long War" from *The Sun My Monument*; to the author and L. Pollinger Ltd.

Laurence Lerner—"What's the Difference?" from *Directions of Memory*; to the author and Messrs. Chatto & Windus Ltd.

John Logan—"The Picnic" from *Ghosts of the Heart* by John Logan; reprinted by permission of the University of Chicago Press.

Archibald MacLeish—"Wildwest" from *Frescoes for Mr. Rockefeller's City*; to the author and Bodley Head Ltd.

Christopher Middleton—"Navaho Children" from *Nonsequences*; to the author and Longmans, Green Ltd.

Wilfred Owen—"Dulce et Decorum Est"; "The Chances" from *Collected Poems*; to the author and Messrs. Chatto & Windus Ltd.

Timothy Palmer—"The Bomb"; to the author.

Peter Porter—"Your Attention Please"; to Scorpion Press.

Henry Reed—"Naming of Parts" from *A Map Of Verona*; to the author and Jonathan Cape Ltd.

Adrienne Rich—"The Evil Eye"; to the author.

Vernon Scannell—"The Fair" from *A Sense of Danger*; to the author and Putnam & Co. Ltd.

Stephen Spender—"My Parents Kept Me" from *My Parents Kept Me*; to the author and Messrs. Faber & Faber.

William Stafford—"Travelling Through the Dark" from *Travelling Through the Dark* by William Stafford. Copyright © 1960 by William Stafford. Reprinted by permission of Messrs. Harper and Row, New York.

Edward Storey—"Cart-Horse Preacher"; to the author.

Dylan Thomas—"The Hunchback in the Park" from *Collected Poems*; to the author and J. M. Dent & Son Ltd. and the Literary Executors of the Dylan Thomas Estate.

R. S. Thomas—"A Peasant"; "January"; "The Lonely Farmer"; "The Poacher"; to the author and Messrs. Rupert Hart-Davis.

Charles Tomlinson—"Mr. Brodsky" from *Poems* and "Winter-Piece" from *A Peopled Landscape*; to the author and Oxford University Press.

Shirley Toulson—"A Photograph"; to the author.

Anthony Thwaite—"Looking On"; "The Boys" from *The Owl In The Tree*; to the author and Oxford University Press.

Arthur Waley (Trans.)—"Protest in the Sixth Year"; "The Orphan" from *Chinese Poems*; to the author and George Allen & Unwin Ltd.

Rex Warner—"Nile Fishermen"; to the author and Bodley Head Ltd.

Y. Yevtushenko—"Lies"; "The Companion"; "Weddings"; to the author and Penguin Books Ltd.

We are also indebted to the Workers' Music Association in their kind help in reproducing the traditional ballads—"The Gresford Disaster"; "I'm Champion at Keepin' 'Em Rollin'"; "Fourpence A Day"; "The Durham Strike"; "The Fireman's Not Me".

Every effort has been made to trace and acknowledge ownership of copyright. The publishers will be glad to make suitable arrangements with any copyright holders whom it has not been possible to contact.

Introduction

THIS anthology represents an attempt to gather together a selection of poetry that will stimulate and interest that wide range of people who are studying in all forms of higher education—I am thinking of those in Technical Colleges of all types, County and Junior Colleges, Colleges of Education and the upper forms of all types of Secondary Schools. It is, I hope, an anthology with a difference, for I have attempted to keep away from the usual kind of poem found in educational anthologies, and to find work that is in touch with the problems of the modern world. For that reason most of the poetry in the book is by modern writers—some of them quite young—but by no means all of it. The established writers are there —Robert Frost, Gerard Manley Hopkins and Thomas Hardy for example—and there is some poetry which is very old indeed. Ballads such as "Johnie Armstrong" and "The Demon Lover" go back several hundred years but are none the less 'modern' for all that.

However, most of the writers are modern writers, and some of their styles of writing and subject-matter may seem very strange to some of you who have been brought up on the more traditional styles of some of the great older poets such as Milton, Wordsworth or Tennyson, yet one must remember that some of these were considered revolutionary in their day. It may be that poems such as "Sometime During Eternity" by Lawrence Ferlinghetti, or "Your Attention Please" by Peter Porter, or "Portrait" by E. E. Cummings will come as a shock to some of you, but this is a good thing, and I am sure that once the immediate strangeness has worn off you will find the subject-matter enjoyable and stimulating.

One aim of this anthology is to show you that poetry can be written in many different styles, and styles which are perhaps more applicable to modern problems than many of the traditional forms, although, of course, the traditional forms of writing are still widely used by many great modern poets and are represented here too.

Another aim is to promote discussion. Many of the poems chosen are not perhaps the best poems that the particular author has written, although in saying that I feel I must add that I do not believe that there is a bad poem in the book; they are chosen because they deal with problems that we meet with in everyday modern life, and many of them are there because I hope they will promote discussion and thought. Questions are raised like that of racial prejudice as for example in Karen Gershon's "Race", or capital punishment as in James Baxter's "A Rope for Harry Fat", or the whole problem of war as in the section headed "The War Game". We see the question of human relationships dealt with in the section, "Light Years Apart", and the complex problem of love from first love in "The Picnic" by John Logan to its break-up as portrayed in the old American ballad, "Frankie and Johnny". The sections themselves are designed to deal with as many aspects of life as possible and I hope there is something for everyone, ending up with some fun in the last one, "Laughs and Afterthoughts", although the afterthoughts may provide a sting in their tail.

The poems are chosen with a wide range of audience in mind, and I trust that everybody—whether they be mechanic, electrician, 'O' or 'A' level candidate, caterer, nurse or student teacher—will find something of value here. I trust too that you will enjoy these poems, for poetry is to be enjoyed, but I also trust that you will be provoked, or annoyed if you like! into talking about them. Finally, I hope that it will help you to see that poetry need not just be about cuckoos, or daffodils, or ethereal women, but can also be about *you* and *your* problems.

ALAN CRANG

SECTION 1
All in a Day's Work

Song of the Wagondriver

My first love was the ten-ton truck
They gave me when I started,
And though she played the bitch with me
I grieved when we were parted.

Since then I've had a dozen more,
The wound was quick to heal,
And now it's easier to say
I'm married to my wheel.

I've trunked it north, I've trunked it south,
On wagons good and bad,
But none was ever really like
The first I ever had.

The life is hard, the hours are long,
Sometimes I cease to feel,
But I go on, for it seems to me
I'm married to my wheel.

Often I think of my home and kids,
Out on the road at night,
And think of taking a local job
Provided the money's right.

Two nights a week I see my wife,
And eat a decent meal,
But otherwise, for all my life,
I'm married to my wheel.

B. S. JOHNSON

John Henry

When John Henry was a little fellow,
  You could hold him in the palm of your hand,
He said to his pa, "When I grow up
  I'm gonna be a steel-drivin' man.
    Gonna be a steel-drivin' man."

One day his captain told him,
  How he had bet a man
That John Henry would beat his steam-drill down,
  'Cos John Henry was the best in the land,
    John Henry was the best in the land.

John Henry kissed the hammer,
  White man turned on steam,
Shaker held John Henry's trusty steel,
  Was the biggest race the world had ever seen,
    Lord, biggest race the world had ever seen.

John Henry on the right side,
  The steam-drill on the left,
"Before I let your steam-drill beat me down,
  I'll hammer my fool self to death,
    Hammer my fool self to death."

Captain heard a mighty rumblin',
  Said, "That mountain must be cavin' in!"
John Henry said to the captain,
  "It's ma hammer swingin' in de wind,
    Ma hammer swingin' in de wind."

John Henry said to his captain,
"Before I ever leave town,
Gimme a twelve pound hammer wid a whale-bone
    handle,
  An' I'll hammer dat steam-driver down,
    I'll hammer dat steam-driver down!"

John Henry said to his captain,
  "Now man ain't nothin' but a man,
But before I'll let dat steam-drill beat me down,
  I'll die wid ma hammer in ma hand,
    Die wid ma hammer in ma hand!"

The man that invented the steam-drill
  He thought he was mighty fine,
John Henry drove down fourteen feet
  While the steam-drill only made nine,
    Steam-drill only made nine!

"Oh, lookaway yonder, captain,
  You can't see like me."
He gave a long an' loud an' lonesome cry,
  "Lawd, that hammer be the death of me,
    Lawd, a hammer be the death of me!"

John Henry hammerin' on de mountain
  As the whistle blew for half-past two,
The last words his captain heard him say,
  "I've done hammered ma insides in two,
    Lawd, I've hammered ma insides in two!"

The hammer that John Henry swung
  It weighed over twelve pound,
He broke a rib in his left-hand side
  An' his intrels fell on de ground,
    An' his intrels fell on de ground.

John Henry, O, John Henry,
  His blood is runnin' red,
Fell right down wid his hammer to the ground,
  Said, "I beat 'im to the bottom but I'm dead,
    Lawd, beat 'im to de bottom but I'm dead."

When John Henry was layin' there dyin',
  The people all by his side,
The very last words they heard him say,
  "Gimme a cool drink of water 'fore I die,
    A cool drink of water 'fore ah die."

They carried him down by de river,
  An' buried him in de sand,
An' everybody that passed that way,
  Said, "There lies that steel-drivin' man,
    Oh Lawd, there lies a steel-drivin' man!"

ANONYMOUS

View of a Pig

The pig lay on a barrow dead.
It weighed, they said, as much as three men.
Its eyes closed, pink white eyelashes.
Its trotters stuck straight out.

Such weight and thick pink bulk
Set in death seemed not just dead.
It was less than lifeless, further off
It was like a sack of wheat.

I thumped it without feeling remorse.
One feels guilty insulting the dead,
Walking on graves. But this pig
Did not seem able to accuse.

It was too dead. Just so much
A poundage of lard and pork.
Its last dignity had entirely gone.
It was not a figure of fun.

Too dead now to pity.
To remember its life, din, stronghold
Of earthly pleasure as it had been,
Seemed a false effort, and off the point.

Too deadly factual. Its weight
Oppressed me—how could it be moved?
And the trouble of cutting it up!
The gash in its throat was shocking, but not pathetic.

Once I ran at a fair in the noise
To catch a greased piglet
That was faster and nimbler than a cat,
Its squeal was the rending of metal.

Pigs must have hot blood, they feel like ovens.
Their bite is worse than a horse's—
They chop a half-moon clean out.
They eat cinders, dead cats.

Distinctions and admirations such
As this one was long finished with.
I stared at it a long time. They were going to scald it,
Scald it and scour it like a doorstep.

TED HUGHES

The Gresford Disaster

You've heard of the Gresford disaster,
  The terrible price that was paid;
Two hundred and forty-two colliers were lost
  And three men of the rescue brigade.

It occurred in the month of September,
  At three in the morning that pit
Was racked by a violent explosion
  In the Dennis where dust lay so thick.

The gas in the Dennis deep section
  Was packed like snow in a drift,
And many a man had to leave the coal-face
  Before he had worked out his shift.

A fortnight before the explosion
  To the shot-firer Tomlinson cried;
"If you fire that shot we'll be all blown to hell!"
  And no one can say that he lied.

The fireman's reports they are missing,
  The records of forty-two days;
The colliery manager had them destroyed
  To cover his criminal ways.

Down there in the dark they are lying,
  They died for nine shillings a day;
They've worked out their shift and it's now they must lie
  In the darkness until Judgement Day.

The Lord Mayor of London's collecting
  To help both the children and wives;

The owners have sent some white lilies
  To pay for the colliers' lives.

Farewell our dear wives and our children,
  Farewell our dear comrades as well;
Don't send your sons in the dark dreary mine,
  They'll be damned like the sinners in hell.

(From A. L. LLOYD's "Come all ye bold miners")

The Lonely Farmer

Poor hill farmer astray in the grass:
There came a movement and he looked up, but
All that he saw was the wind pass.
There was a sound of voices on the air,
But where, where? It was only the glib stream talking
Softly to itself. And once when he was walking
Along a lane in spring he was deceived
By a shrill whistle coming through the leaves:
Wait a minute, wait a minute—four swift notes;
He turned, and it was nothing, only a thrush
In the thorn bushes easing its throat.
He swore at himself for paying heed,
The poor hill farmer, so often again
Stopping, staring, listening, in vain,
His ear betrayed by the heart's need.

R. S. THOMAS

I'm Champion at Keeping 'Em Rolling

I am an old timer, I travel the road;
  I sit on me wagon and lumber me load;
My hotel is the jungle, a caf's me abode
  And I'm well-known to Blondie and Mary.
My liquor is diesel-oil laced with strong tea,
  The old highway-code was my first ABC.
And I cut my eyeteeth on an old A.E.C.,
  And I'm champion at keeping 'em rolling.

I've sat in my cabin and broiled in the sun,
  Been snowed up on Shap on the Manchester run;
I've crawled through the fog with my twenty-two tons
  Of fish that was stinking like blazes.
From London to Glasgow, to Newcastle Quay,
  From Liverpool, Preston and Bristol City,
The polones on the road give the thumb-sign to me
  For I'm champion at keeping 'em rolling.

You may sing of your soldiers and sailors so bold
  But there's many and many a hero untold
Who sits at the wheel in the heat and the cold,
  Day after day without sleeping.
So watch out for cops and slow down at the bends,
  Check all your gauges and watch your big-ends,
And zig with your lights when you pass an old friend,
  You'll be champion at keeping 'em rolling.

EWAN MCCOLL

Ambulances

Closed like confessionals, they thread
Loud noons of cities, giving back
None of the glances they absorb.
Light glossy grey, arms on a plaque,
They come to rest at any kerb:
All streets in time are visited.

Then children strewn on steps or road,
Or women coming from the shops
Past smells of different dinners, see
A wild white face that overtops
Red stretcher-blankets momently
As it is carried in and stowed,

And sense the solving emptiness
That lies just under all we do,
And for a second get it whole,
So permanent and blank and true.
The fastened doors recede. "Poor soul,"
They whisper at their own distress;

For borne away in deadened air
May go the sudden shut of loss
Round something nearly at an end,
And what cohered in it across
The years, the unique random blend
Of families and fashions, there

At last begin to loosen. Far
From the exchange of love to lie
Unreachable inside a room

The traffic parts to let go by
Brings closer what is left to come,
And dulls to distance all we are.

PHILIP LARKIN

Fourpence a Day

The ore is waiting in the tubs, the snow's upon the fell;
Canny folk are sleeping yet but lead is reet to sell.
Come, me little washer lad, come, let's away,
We're bound down to slav'ry for fourpence a day.

It's early in the morning, we rise at five o'clock,
And the little slaves come to the door to knock, knock, knock.
Come, me little washer lad, come, let's away,
It's very hard to work for fourpence a day.

My father was a miner and lived down in the town;
'Twas hard work and poverty that always kept him down.
He aimed for me to go to school but brass he couldn't pay,
So I had to go to the washing rake for fourpence a day.

My mother rises out of bed with tears on her cheeks,
Puts my wallet on my shoulders which has to serve a week.
It often fills her great big heart when she unto me does say,
"I never thought thou would have worked for fourpence a day."

Fourpence a day, me lad, and very hard to work
And never a pleasant look from a gruffy looking Turk.
His conscience it may fail and his heart it may give way,
Then he'll raise our wages to ninepence a day.

(From JOHN GOWLAND's singing, a retired lead miner)

Elegy for Alfred Hubbard

Hubbard is dead, the old plumber;
who will mend our burst pipes now,
the tap that has dripped all the summer,
testing the sink's overflow?

No other like him. Young men with knowledge
of new techniques, theories from books,
may better his work straight from college,
but who will challenge his squint-eyed looks

in kitchen, bathroom, under floorboards,
rules of thumb which were often wrong;
seek as erringly stopcocks in cupboards,
or make a job last half as long?

He was a man who knew the ginnels,
alleyways, streets—the whole district,
family secrets, minor annals,
time-honoured fictions fused to fact.

Seventy years of gossip muttered
under his cap, his tufty thatch,
so that his talk was slow and clotted,
hard to follow, and too much.

As though nothing fell, none vanished,
and time were the maze of Cheetham Hill,
in which the dead—with jobs unfinished—
waited to hear him ring the bell.

For much he never got round to doing,
but meant to, when weather bucked up,
or worsened, or when his pipe was drawing,
or when he'd finished this cup.

I thought time, he forgot so often,
had forgotten him, but here's Death's pomp
over his house, and by the coffin
the son who will inherit his blowlamp,

tools, workshop, cart, and cornet
(pride of Cheetham Prize Brass Band),
and there's his mourning widow, Janet,
stood at the gate he'd promised to mend.

Soon he will make his final journey;
shaved and silent, strangely trim,
with never a pause to talk to any-
body: how arrow-like, for him!

In St. Mark's Church, whose dismal tower
he pointed and painted when a lad,
they will sing his praises amidst flowers
while, somewhere, a cellar starts to flood,

and the housewife banging his front-door knocker
is not surprised to find him gone,
and runs for Thwaite, who's a better worker,
and sticks at a job until it's done.

TONY CONNOR

Out, Out

The buzz-saw snarled and rattled in the yard
And made dust and dropped stove-length sticks of wood,
Sweet-scented stuff when the breeze drew across it.
And from there those that lifted eyes could count
Five mountain ranges one behind the other
Under the sunset far into Vermont.
And the saw snarled and rattled, snarled and rattled,
As it ran light, or had to bear a load.
And nothing happened: day was all but done.
Call it a day, I wish they might have said
To please the boy by giving him the half hour
That a boy counts so much when saved from work.
His sister stood beside them in her apron
To tell them "Supper". At the word, the saw,
As if to prove saws knew what supper meant,
Leaped out at the boy's hand, or seemed to leap—
He must have given the hand. However it was,
Neither refused the meeting. But the hand!
The boy's first outcry was a rueful laugh.
As he swung toward them holding up the hand
Half in appeal, but half as if to keep
The life from spilling. Then the boy saw all—
Since he was old enough to know, big boy
Doing a man's work, though child at heart—
He saw all spoiled. "Don't let him cut my hand off—
The doctor, when he comes. Don't let him, sister!"
So. But the hand was gone already.
The doctor put him in the dark of ether.
He lay and puffed his lips out with his breath.
And then—the watcher at his pulse took fright.
No one believed. They listened at his heart.

Little—less—nothing!—and that ended it.
No more to build on there. And they, since they
Were not the one dead, turned to their affairs.

ROBERT FROST

SECTION 2

Barriers

Mending Wall

Something there is that doesn't love a wall,
That sends the frozen-ground-swell under it,
And spills the upper boulders in the sun;
And makes gaps even two can pass abreast.
The work of hunters is another thing:
I have come after them and made repair
Where they have left not one stone on a stone,
But they would have the rabbit out of hiding,
To please the yelping dogs. The gaps I mean,
No one has seen them made or heard them made,
But at spring mending-time we find them there.
I let my neighbour know beyond the hill;
And on a day we meet to walk the line
And set the wall between us once again.
We keep the wall between us as we go.
To each the boulders that have fallen to each.
And some are loaves and some so nearly balls
We have to use a spell to make them balance:
"Stay where you are until our backs are turned!"
We wear our fingers rough with handling them.
Oh, just another kind of outdoor game,
One on a side. It comes to little more:
There where it is we do not need the wall:
He is all pine and I am apple orchard.
My apple trees will never get across
And eat the cones under his pines, I tell him.
He only says, "Good fences make good neighbours."
Spring is the mischief in me, and I wonder
If I could put a notion in his head:
"*Why* do they make good neighbours? Isn't it

Where there are cows? But here there are no cows.
Before I built a wall I'd ask to know
What I was walling in or walling out,
And to whom I was like to give offence.
Something there is that doesn't love a wall,
That wants it down." I could say "Elves" to him,
But it's not elves exactly, and I'd rather
He said it for himself. I see him there
Bringing a stone grasped firmly by the top
In each hand, like an old-stone savage armed.
He moves in darkness as it seems to me,
Not of woods only and the shade of trees.
He will not go behind his father's saying,
And he likes having thought of it so well
He says again, "Good fences make good neighbours."

ROBERT FROST

Race

When I returned to my home town
believing that no-one would care
who I was and what I thought
it was as if the people caught
an echo of me everywhere
they knew my story by my face
and I who am always alone
became a symbol of my race

Like every living Jew I have
in imagination seen
the gas-chamber the mass-grave
the unknown body which was mine

and found in every German face
behind the mask the mark of Cain
I will not make their thoughts my own
by hating people for their race

KAREN GERSHON

My Parents Kept Me from Children Who Were Rough

My parents kept me from children who were rough
Who threw words like stones and who wore torn clothes.
Their thighs showed through rags. They ran in the street
And climbed cliffs and stripped by the country streams.

I feared more than tigers their muscles like iron
Their jerking hands and their knees tight on my arms.
I feared the salt coarse pointing of those boys
Who copied my lisp behind me on the road.

They were lithe, they sprang out behind hedges
Like dogs to bark at my world. They threw mud
While I looked the other way, pretending to smile.
I longed to forgive them, but they never smiled.

STEPHEN SPENDER

The Durham Strike

In our Durham County I am sorry for to say,
That hunger and starvation is increasing every day.
For the want of food and coals we know not what to do,
But with your kind assistance we will see the battle thro'.

I need not state the reason why we've been brought so low;
The masters have behaved unkind, which everyone will know,
Because we won't lie doon and let them tret us as they like,
To punish us they've stopped the pits and caused the present strike.

The pulley wheels have ceased to move which went so swift
    aroond,
The horses and the ponies, too, all brought from undergroond.
Our work is taken from us and they care not if we die,
For they can eat the best of food and drink the best when dry.

The miner and his wife, too, each mornin' have to roam,
To seek for bread to feed the hungry little ones at home.
The flour barrel is empty now, their true and faithful friend,
Which makes the thousands wish today the strike was at an end.

Well, let them stand or let them lie or do whatever they choose,—
To give them thirteen and a half we ever shall refuse!
They're always willin' to receive but not inclined to give,
And very soon they won't allow a workin' man to live.

The miners of Northumberland we shall forever praise,
For being so kind in helpin' us these tyrannisin' days.
We thank the other counties, too, that have been doin' the same,
For every man who hears this song will know we're not to blame.

(From A. L. LLOYD's "Come all ye bold miners")

Protest in the Sixth Year of Ch'ien Fu
(A.D. 879)

The hills and rivers of the lowland country
  You have made your battle-ground.
How do you suppose the people who live there
  Will procure "firewood and hay"?
Do not let me hear you talking together
  About titles and promotions;
For a single general's reputation
  Is made out of ten thousand corpses.

TS'AO SUNG, translated by ARTHUR WALEY

Flute Player

On Sundays they often go by—
The thin, blank boy leans over his flute,
His shoulders announcing: BLIND.
Notes, careful and isolated, grope
Towards the shape of a hymn, a popular song
And another hymn: it is Sunday, after all.
Money falls down from expensive flats
And tasteful bed-sitters. And the fat old man,
Genial and bowing, holds out a dirty hat.

The spring drifts by.
If the lad's coat is shabbier, he would not know.
But the flute blossoms into some pattern now—
A new folk-song, a sadder air;
I detect a bit of Bach. We spin a minor summer coin
To the old man in his smart new jacket.

Today, as they pass by,
It seems as though music, golden as the autumn,
Eddies between the bed-sitters and the expensive flats.
And largesse, compassion, conscience-money
Tinkle on the pavement. Yet is there anything here—
In these perfect phrases—of love, of despair,
Of laughter? No, there is only a thin, blank boy
And a column of sound, pure as a tuning fork,
Spiralling correctly into the air.
So why do I still throw down my shillings
To pay for that fat old man's cigar?

A. C. BOYD

The Poor Wake Up Quickly

Surprised at night,
The trishaw driver
Slithers from the carriage,
Hurls himself upon the saddle.

With what violence he peddles
Slapbang into the swarming night,
Neon skidding off his cheekbones!
Madly he makes away
In the wrong direction.
I tap his shoulder nervously.
Madly he turns about
Between the taxis and the trams,
Makes away electric-eyed
In another wrong direction.

How do I star in that opium dream?
A hulking red-faced ruffian
Who beats him on his bony back,
Cursing in the tongue of demons.

But when we're there
He grumbles mildly over his wage,
Like a sober man,
A man who has had no recent visions.
The poor wake up quickly.

D. J. ENRIGHT

Sometime During Eternity

Sometime during eternity
                         some guys show up
and one of them
            who shows up real late
                              is a kind of carpenter
    from some square-type place
                      like Galilee
    and he starts wailing
                  and claiming he is hip
      to who made heaven
                    and earth
                        and that the cat
      who really laid it on us
                      is his Dad
  And moreover
    he adds
          It's all writ down
                          on some scroll-type parchments
      which some henchmen
            leave lying around the Dead Sea somewheres
          a long time ago
                      and which you won't even find
  for a coupla thousand years or so
                          or at least for

nineteen hundred and fortyseven
                              of them
               to be exact
                    and even then
          nobody really believes them
                         or me
                              for that matter
     You're hot
               they tell him
     And they cool him
     They stretch him on the Tree to cool
          And everybody after that
                              is always making models
               of this Tree
                    with Him hung up
     and always crooning His name
                         and calling Him to come down
               and sit in
                    on their combo
          as if he is *the* king cat
                    who's got to blow
          or they can't quite make it
     Only he don't come down
                         from His Tree
Him just hang there
               on His Tree
                    looking real Petered out
               and real cool
                         and also
          according to a roundup
                    of late world news
     from the usual unreliable sources
                    real dead.

                         LAWRENCE FERLINGHETTI

Wildwest

There were none of my blood in this battle:
There were Minneconjous: Sans Arcs: Brules:
Many nations of Sioux: they were few men galloping:

This would have been in the long days in June:
They were galloping well deployed under the plum-trees:
They were driving riderless horses: themselves they were few:

Crazy Horse had done it with few numbers:
Crazy Horse was small for a Lakota:
He was riding always alone thinking of something:

He was standing alone by the picket lines by the ropes:
He was young then: he was thirty when he died:
Unless there were children to talk he took no notice:

When the soldiers came for him there on the other side
On the Greasy Grass in the villages we were shouting
"Hoka Hey! Crazy Horse will be riding!"

They fought in the water: horses and men were drowning:
They rode on the butte: dust settled in the sunlight:
Hoka Hey! they lay on the bloody ground:

No one could tell of the dead which man was Custer . . .
That was the end of his luck: by that river:
The soldiers beat him at Slim Buttes once:

They beat him at Willow Creek when the snow lifted:
The last time they beat him was the Tongue:
He had only the meat he had made and of that little:

Do you ask why he should fight? It was his country:
My God should he not fight? It was his:
But after the Tongue there were no herds to be hunting:

He cut the knots of the tails and he led them in:
He cried out "I am Crazy Horse! Do not touch me!"
There were many soldiers between and the gun glinting. . . .

And a Mister Josiah Perham of Maine had much of the
land Mister Perham was building the Northern Pacific
railroad that is Mister Perham was saying at lunch that

Forty say fifty millions of acres in gift and
government grant outright ought to be worth a
wide price on the Board at two-fifty and

Later a Mister Cooke had relieved Mister Perham and
later a Mister Morgan relieved Mister Cooke.
Mister Morgan converted at prices current:

It was all prices to them: they never looked at it:
why should they look at the land: they were Empire Builders:
it was all in the bid and the asked and the ink on their books . . .

When Crazy Horse was there by the Black Hills
His heart would be big with the love he had for that country
And all the game he had seen and the mares he had ridden

And how it went out from you wide and clean in the sunlight

ARCHIBALD MACLEISH
(From "Frescoes for Mr. Rockerfeller's City")

Lies

Telling lies to the young is wrong.
Proving to them that lies are true is wrong.
Telling them that God's in his heaven
and all's well with the world is wrong.
The young know what you mean. The young are people.
Tell them the difficulties can't be counted,
and let them see not only what will be
but see with clarity these present times.
Say obstacles exist they must encounter
sorrow happens, hardship happens.
The hell with it. Who never knew
the price of happiness will not be happy.
Forgive no error you recognize,
it will repeat itself, increase,
and afterwards our pupils
will not forgive in us what we forgave.

                                Y. YEVTUSHENKO

Unmarried Mothers

In the Convent of the Sacred Heart,
The Long Room has been decorated
Where a Bishop can dine off golden plate:
As Oriental Potentate.
Girls, who will never wheel a go-cart,
Cook, sew, wash, dig, milk cows, clean stables
And, twice a day, giving their babes
The teat, herdlike, yield milk that cost

Them dearly, when their skirts were tossed up
Above their haunches. Hook or zip
Has warded them at Castlepollard.
Luckier girls, on board a ship,
Watch new hope spraying from the bollard.

AUSTIN CLARKE

Cardoness Castle

(Adm. 6d; 10–4, Sun. from 2) a splendid 15th cent. tower (View)

The keeper stopped the mower on the lawn,
Pocketed a stray dead leaf, sixpence, and
Our compliments on his neat gardens, graciously,
And led us to the ramp. Here in a siege
They brought the horses in; here were the stores;
And once the sea came to the very motte.
Romantic, noble pile; we gazed and saw
Appropriate horsemen, rugged warriors,
Clan proud to war with clan, historic ghosts

But these too literary unrealities stayed there outside
Beneath the Ministry signs about the monument.

Inside we took a tour of human evil: here
Above the door a grating: small greedy brutes
Lured in their confidences, and then split their skulls
Or charred their guests' brains out with molten lead.
Step further: in the wall a privy, out
So that one ostler sat above another, jeering, near
An oubliette, where, dropped fifteen feet down,
Languished the captured enemy, oppressed, evicted—

With "dangerous" ideas—and through the castle wall
A hole at which they dangled rich hot food
To taunt those dying, or extract by thirst
"Confessions", secret names—and then destroyed
The turncoat wretches. From the vertiginous tower
Numbers had been thrown: before the stone fireplace
Dark wiry bloodsoaked men had writhed in pain
Whom no despairing linen-tearing lady there could save,
While from the slits shot arrows into trunks, while
Maid-servants cowered in sweaty rush-floored rooms,
And rats slid hungrily from enemy to tower
Where spilt blood, oatmeal, gunpowder and wine
Ran to the seadrains from the suffering cruel
Dangerous brown men, howling their uncouth tongue.

We came out in the sunlight where the grass
Shaved short, a harmless green, hid decayed pits and graves
Where lay those creatures' bones. And could pretend
Life was now orderly and neat, with flowers:
No daggers at our throats, no human herds
Unprivate closeted in exhausted keep alcoves.

Till we took up our morning newspaper
In the car, with the maps, again, and saw
THREE IN A PRISON CELL: on the same page, VICTIMS' HANDS
TROPHIES IN TRIBESMEN'S BELTS, and everywhere
More perfect treachery, without such weathered stones,
Protecting purlieus by poisoning the marrow in all bones.

DAVID HOLBROOK

Bomb

No, I don't seem to be very pre-
Occupied with the
Bomb, do
I?
It isn't that I don't care—after all, none
Of us want to be blasted to
Kingdom Come, do
We?—it's
Just that Gaye is prettier and a much nicer
Shape than a
Mushroom.
And then there's not much one
Person can
Do about it and there'll be all
Eternity to think about what we
Could have
Done.
Gaye. Isn't she
Sweet?
I'd go and call her now, but I've
Forgotten the
Number, and we're not on the
Phone and I'd
Probably be blasted to bits before I
Got to the
Call-box.

TIMOTHY PALMER

Blues for the Hitch-hiking Dead:
Last Chorus of Thirty-three

It was three stories
in Notting Hill—

The ground floored
by working people
On Her Majesty's Service—
They had no use for marching
in favour of banning the bomb
    —if the Queen went
    England was sunk.
They minded their business
    —went about it rather
with a D'you mind if anyone
so much as brushed past them
    on the way up—

The first housed
thirteen exiles
all sizes shapes and colours, disgusting
    always parties and one hell
of a lot of noise—that terrible music
    hysterical fusses
Nobody sat next to them on buses;
each made a little order for himself
or herself or each other and
    their animals and
    such a lot of rubbish—

and as for the couple on top—well,
They were just plain degenerate

—Why, those two were all ways in out
upstairs downstairs in the middle—yes
they had a lot of truck with the bloody foreigners
above the basement and below the stairs
—trying to keep in step
    never quite making it
because so much involved with the rest—

The groundlings don't bother with them
    apart from clandestine mockery
      —except when they're interfered with
That's when the trouble starts—

    and now the bomb has fallen
    and broken all our hearts

MICHAEL HOROVITZ

Poetry of Departures

Sometimes you hear, fifth-hand,
As epitaph:
"He chucked up everything
And just cleared off,"
And always the voice will sound
Certain you approve
This audacious, purifying,
Elemental move.

And they are right, I think.
We all hate home
And having to be there:
I detest my room,

Its specially-chosen junk,
The good books, the good bed,
And my life, in perfect order:
So to hear it said

"He walked out on the whole crowd"
Leaves me flushed and stirred,
Like "Then she undid her dress"
Or "take that you bastard";
Surely I can, if he did?
And that helps me stay
Sober and industrious.
But I'd go today,

Yes, swagger the nut-strewn roads,
Crouch in the fo'c'sle
Stubbly with goodness, if
It weren't so artificial,
Such a deliberate step backwards
To create an object:
Books; china; a life
Reprehensibly perfect.

PHILIP LARKIN

Let Us Be Men—

For God's sake, let us be men
not monkeys minding machines
or sitting with your tails curled
while the machine amuses us, the radio or film or gramophone.

Monkeys with a bland grin on our faces.—

D. H. LAWRENCE

SECTION 3

Characters All

Cart-horse Preacher

It would have been no use
using the smooth liturgical words
of a cosy religion;
his congregation left their work
in the wet fields of the fen-country,
their cracked hands swollen
with beet-chopping.

To have asked them into the stiff pews
of a cold church would have meant
shouting at air; he knew
the hollow stillness of that place
left them more frozen than the fields,
and holy whining more than winter
lined their face.

So he gathered them round him
on the market square, saying
"I'll speak a language you can understand,
who cares about the lovely use of words
when half the words are nothing more than sound".
Their frost-blue ears were tingled
by his fire.

They met him every Sunday-night and knew
God would be called a muck-heap
or a cow, and no irreverence meant.
"Crops thrive" he'd say, "where muck is spread,
and milk pumps life in every sucker's mouth".
He solved the mystery of their fields,
healed their backs.

But now he's dead, and God's
locked in His church, stiff and alone.
Men work their days out on the land
wondering why the old cart-horse preacher
bothered them at all. Sometimes they feel
without him frost stays longer in their hands
and limbs more often ache.

EDWARD STOREY

Mr. Brodsky

I had heard
before, of an
American who would have preferred
to be an Indian;
but not
until Mr. Brodsky, of one
whose professed and long
pondered-on passion
was to become a Scot,
who even sent for haggis and oatcakes
across continent.
Having read him
in Cambridge English
a verse or two
from MacDiarmid,
I was invited
to repeat the reading
before a Burns Night Gathering
where the Balmoral Pipers
of Albuquerque would
play in the haggis

out of its New York tin.
Of course, I said
No. No, I could *not* go
and then
half-regretted I had not been.
But to console
and cure the wish, came
Mr. Brodsky, bringing
his pipes and played
until the immense, distended
bladder of leather seemed
it could barely contain its water—
tears (idle
tears) for the bridal of Annie Laurie
and Morton J. Brodsky.
A bagpipe in a dwelling is
a resonant instrument
and there he stood
lost in the gorse
the heather or whatever
six thousand
miles and more
from the infection's source,
in our neo-New Mexican parlour
where I had heard
before of an
American who would have preferred
to be merely an Indian.

CHARLES TOMLINSON

Felix Randal

Felix Randal the farrier, O he is dead then? my duty all ended
Who have watched his mould of man, big-boned and hardy-
  handsome
Pining, pining, till time when reason rambled in it and some
Fatal four disorders, fleshed there, all contended?
Sickness broke him. Impatient he cursed at first, but mended
Being anointed and all; though a heavenlier heart began some
Months earlier, since I had our sweet reprieve and ransom
Tendered to him. Ah well, God rest him all road ever he offended!

This seeing the sick endears them to us, us too it endears.
My tongue had taught thee comfort, touch had quenched thy tears,
Thy tears that touched my heart, child, Felix, poor Felix Randal;

How far from then forethought of, all thy more boistrous years,
When thou at the random grim forge, powerful amidst peers,
Didst fettle for the great grey drayhorse his bright and battering
  sandal!

GERARD MANLEY HOPKINS

To My Mother

Most near, most dear, most loved and most far,
Under the window where I often found her
Sitting as huge as Asia, seismic with laughter,
Gin and chicken helpless in her Irish hand,
Irresistible as Rabelais, but most tender for
The lame dogs and hurt birds that surround her,—
She is a procession no one can follow after
But be like a little dog following a brass band.

She will not glance up at the bomber, or condescend
To drop her gin and scuttle to a cellar,
But lean on the mahogany table like a mountain
Whom only faith can move, and so I send
O all my faith and all my love to tell her
That she will move from mourning into morning.

GEORGE BARKER

Timothy Winters

Timothy Winters comes to school
With eyes as wide as a football-pool,
Ears like bombs and teeth like splinters:
A blitz of a boy is Timothy Winters.

His belly is white, his neck is dark,
And his hair is an exclamation mark.
His clothes are enough to scare a crow
And through his britches the blue winds blow.

When teacher talks he won't hear a word
And he shoots down dead the arithmetic-bird,
He licks the patterns off his plate
And he's not even heard of the Welfare State.

Timothy Winters has bloody feet
And he lives in a house on Suez Street,
He sleeps in a sack on the kitchen floor
And they say there aren't boys like him any more.

Old man Winters likes his beer
And his missus ran off with a bombardier,
Grandma sits in the grate with a gin
And Timothy's dosed with an aspirin.

The Welfare Worker lies awake
But the law's as tricky as a ten-foot snake,
So Timothy Winters drinks his cup
And slowly goes on growing up.

At Morning Prayers the Headmaster helves
For children less fortunate than ourselves,
And the loudest response in the room is when
Timothy Winters roars "Amen!"

So come one angel, come on ten:
Timothy Winters says "Amen
Amen amen amen amen."
Timothy Winters, Lord.
                    Amen.

                        CHARLES CAUSLEY

The Zulu Girl

When in the sun the hot red acres smoulder,
Down where the sweating gang its labour plies,
A girl flings down her hoe, and from her shoulder
Unslings her child tormented by the flies.

She takes him to a ring of shadow pooled
By thorn-trees: purpled with the blood of ticks,
While her sharp nails, in slow caresses ruled,
Prowl through his hair with sharp electric clicks,

His sleepy mouth, plugged by the heavy nipple,
Tugs like a puppy, grunting as he feeds:
Through his frail nerves her own deep languors ripple
Like a broad river sighing through its reeds.

Yet in that drowsy stream his flesh imbibes
An old unquenched unsmotherable heat—
The curbed ferocity of beaten tribes,
The sullen dignity of their defeat.

Her body looms above him like a hill
Within whose shade a village lies at rest,
Or the first cloud so terrible and still
That bears the coming harvest in its breast.

ROY CAMPBELL

Portrait

Buffalo Bill's
defunct
     who used to
     ride a watersmooth-silver
                     stallion
and break onetwothreefourfive—pigeonsjustlikethat
                                 Jesus
he was a handsome man
                and what i want to know is
how do you like your blueeyed boy
Mister Death

E. E. CUMMINGS

Six Young Men

The celluloid of a photograph holds them well,—
Six young men, familiar to their friends.
Four decades that have faded and ochre-tinged
This photograph have not wrinkled the faces or the hands.
Though their cocked hats are not now fashionable,
Their shoes shine. One imparts an intimate smile,
One chews a grass, one lowers his eyes, bashful,
One is ridiculous with cocky pride—
Six months after this picture they were all dead.

All are trimmed for a Sunday jaunt. I know
That bilberried bank, that thick tree, that black wall,
Which are there yet and not changed. From where these sit
You hear the water of seven streams fall
To the roarer in the bottom, and through all
The leafy valley a rumouring of air go.
Pictured here, their expressions listen yet,
And still that valley has not changed its sound
Though their faces are four decades under the ground.

This one was shot in an attack and lay
Calling in the wire, then this one, his best friend,
Went out to bring him in and was shot too;
And this one, the very moment he was warned
From potting at tin-cans in no-man's-land,
Fell back dead with his rifle-sights shot away.
The rest, nobody knows what they came to,
But come to the worst they must have done, and held it
Closer than their hope; all were killed.

Here see a man's photograph,
The locket of a smile, turned overnight
Into the hospital of his mangled last
Agony and hours; see bundled in it
His mightier-than-a-man dead bulk and weight:
And on this one place which keeps him alive
(In his Sunday best) see fall war's worst
Thinkable flash and rending, onto his smile
Forty years rotting into soil.

That man's not more alive whom you confront
And shake by the hand, see hale, hear speak loud,
Than any of these six celluloid smiles are,
Nor prehistoric or fabulous beast more dead;
No thought so vivid as their smoking blood;
To regard this photograph might well dement,
Such contradictory permanent horrors here
Smile from the single exposure and shoulder out
One's own body from its instant and heat.

TED HUGHES

A Peasant

Iago Prytherch his name, though, be it allowed,
Just an ordinary man of the bald Welsh hills,
Who pens a few sheep in a gap of cloud.
Docking mangels, chipping the green skin
From the yellow bones with a half-witted grin
Of satisfaction, or churning the crude earth
To a stiff sea of clods that glint in the wind—
So are his days spent, his spittled mirth
Rarer than the sun that cracks the cheeks

Of the gaunt sky perhaps once in a week.
And then at night see him fixed in his chair
Motionless, except when he leans to gob in the fire.
There is something frightening in the vacancy of his mind.
His clothes, sour with years of sweat
And animal contact, shock the refined,
But affected, sense with their stark naturalness.
Yet this is your prototype, who, season by season
Against siege of rain and the wind's attrition,
Preserves his stock, an impregnable fortress
Not to be stormed even in death's confusion.
Remember him, then, for he, too, is a winner of wars,
Enduring like a tree under the curious stars.

R. S. THOMAS

Child's Bouncing Song

Molly Vickers
wets her knickers,
Georgie's father's big and black,
cream on Sunday
milk on Monday,
I'm the cock of all the back.

Tell me whose a
bigger boozer
Mister Baker beats them all,
from his lorry
watch him hurry,
touch the ground and touch the wall.

Who're the gentry
down our entry—
Mrs. Smith's got two T.V.'s.
What if her coat
is a fur coat,
all her kids are full of fleas.

Joan loves Harry,
Jack will marry
Edna when they both grow up,
I'll announce it,
bounce bounce bounce it,
our dog Whiskers' had a pup.

High and low and
to and fro and
down the street and up the hill,
Mrs. Cuthbert's
husband snuffed it,
she got nothing from his will.

Mister, mister,
Shirley's sister
won a prize on Blackpool prom,
mam'll smother
our kid brother
when the school inspectors come.

Skip and hopping
I'm off shopping,
Tuesday night it's pie for tea,
please to take this
ball and make this
song of bouncing song for me.

TONY CONNOR

Elvis Presley

Two minutes long it pitches through some bar:
Unreeling from a corner box, the sigh
Of this one, in his gangling finery
And crawling sideburns, wielding a guitar.

The limitations where he found success
Are ground on which he, panting, stretches out
In turn, promiscuously, by every note.
Our idiosyncrasy and likeness.

We keep ourselves in touch with a mere dime:
Distorting hackneyed words in hackneyed songs
He turns revolt into a style, prolongs
The impulse to a habit of the time.

Whether he poses or is real, no cat
Bothers to say: the pose held is a stance,
Which, generation of the very chance
It wars on, may be posture for combat.

THOM   GUNN

SECTION 4
The War Game

Your Attention, Please

The Polar DEW has just warned that
A nuclear rocket strike of
At least one thousand megatons
Has been launched by the enemy
Directly at our major cities.
This announcement will take
Two and a quarter minutes to make,
You therefore have a further
Eight and a quarter minutes
To comply with the shelter
Requirements published in the Civil
Defence Code—section Atomic Attack.
A specially shortened Mass
Will be broadcast at the end
Of this announcement—
Protestant and Jewish services
Will begin simultaneously—
Select your wavelength immediately
According to instructions
In the Defence Code. Do not
Take well-loved pets (including birds)
Into your shelter—they will consume
Fresh air. Leave the old and bed-
ridden, you can do nothing for them.
Remember to press the sealing
Switch when everyone is in
The shelter. Set the radiation
Aerial, turn on the geiger barometer.
Turn off your Television now.
Turn off your radio immediately
The Services end. At the same time

Secure explosion plugs in the ears
Of each member of your family. Take
Down your plasma flasks. Give your children
The pills marked one and two
In the C.D. green container, then put
Them to bed. Do not break
The inside airlock seals until
The radiation All Clear shows
(Watch for the cuckoo in your
perspex panel), or your District
Touring Doctor rings your bell.
If before this, your air becomes
Exhausted or if any of your family
Is critically injured, administer
The capsules marked "Valley Forge"
(Red pocket in No. 1 Survival Kit)
For painless death. (Catholics
Will have been instructed by their priests
What to do in this eventuality.)
This announcement is ending. Our President
Has already given orders for
Massive retaliation—it will be
Decisive. Some of us may die.
Remember, statistically
It is not likely to be you.
All flags are flying fully dressed
On Government buildings—the sun is shining.
Death is the least we have to fear.
We are all in the hands of God,
Whatever happens happens by His Will.
Now go quickly to your shelters.

PETER PORTER

Dulce et Decorum Est

Bent double, like old beggars under sacks,
Knock-kneed, coughing like hags, we cursed through sludge,
Till on the haunting flares we turned our backs,
And towards our distant rest began to trudge.
Men marched asleep. Many had lost their boots,
But limped on, blood-shod. All went lame, all blind;
Drunk with fatigue; deaf even to the hoots
Of gas-shells dropping softly behind.

Gas! Gas! Quick, boys!—An ecstasy of fumbling,
Fitting the clumsy helmets just in time,
But someone still was yelling out and stumbling
And floundering like a man in fire or lime.—
Dim through the misty panes and thick green light,
As under a green sea, I saw him drowning.

In all my dreams before my helpless sight
He plunges at me, guttering, choking, drowning.

If in some smothering dreams, you too could pace
Behind the wagon that we flung him in,
And watch the white eyes writhing in his face,
His hanging face, like a devil's sick of sin;
If you could hear, at every jolt, the blood
Come gargling from the froth-corrupted lungs,
Bitter as the cud
Of vile, incurable sores on innocent tongues—
My friend, you would not tell with such high zest
To children ardent for some desperate glory,
The old lie: Dulce et decorum est
Pro patria mori.

WILFRED OWEN

The Fifth Sense

A 65-year-old Cypriot Greek shepherd, Nicolis Loizou, was
wounded by security forces early today. He was challenged twice;
when he failed to answer, troops opened fire. A subsequent hospital
examination showed that the man was deaf. (NEWS ITEM, 30th
December, 1957.)

Lamps burn all the night
Here, where people must be watched and seen,
And I, a shepherd, Nicolis Loizou,
Wish for the dark, for I have been
Sure-footed in the dark, but now my sight
Stumbles among these beds, scattered white boulders,
As I lean towards my far slumbering house
With the night lying upon my shoulders.

My sight was always good,
Better than others. I could taste wine and bread
And name the field they spattered when the harvest
Broke. I could coil in the red
Scent of the fox out of a maze of wood
And grass. I could touch mist, I could touch breath.
But of my sharp senses I had only four.
The fifth one pinned me to my death.

The soldiers must have called
The word they needed: Halt. Not hearing it,
I was their failure, relaxed against the winter
Sky, the flag of their defeat.
With their five senses they could not have told
That I lacked one, and so they had to shoot.
They would fire at a rainbow if it had
A colour less than they were taught.

Christ said that when one sheep
Was lost, the rest meant nothing any more.
Here in this hospital, where others' breathing
Swings like a lantern in the polished floor
And squeezes those who cannot sleep,
I see how precious each thing is, how dear,
For I may never touch, smell, taste, or see
Again, because I could not hear.

PATRICIA BEER

The Man He Killed

"Had he and I but met
    By some old ancient inn,
We should have sat us down to wet
    Right many a nipperkin!

"But ranged as infantry,
    And staring face to face,
I shot at him as he at me,
    And killed him in his place.

"I shot him dead because—
    Because he was my foe,
Just so: my foe of course he was;
    That's clear enough; although

"He thought he'd 'list, perhaps,
    Off-hand like—just as I—
Was out of work—had sold his traps—
    No other reason why.

"Yes; quaint and curious war is!
You shoot a fellow down
You'd treat if met where any bar is,
Or help to half a crown."

THOMAS HARDY

The Companion

She was sitting on the rough embankment,
her cape too big for her tied on slapdash
over an odd little hat with a bobble on it,
her eyes brimming with tears of hopelessness.
An occasional butterfly floated down
fluttering warm wings onto the rails.
The clinkers under foot were deep lilac.
We got cut off from our grandmothers
while the Germans were dive-bombing the train.
Katya was her name. She was nine.
I'd no idea what I could do about her,
but doubt quickly dissolved to certainty:
I'd have to take this thing under my wing;
—girls were in some sense of the word human,
a human being couldn't be just left.
The droning in the air and the explosions
receded farther into the distance,
I touched the little girl on her elbow.
"Come on. Do you hear? What are you waiting for?"
The world was big and we were not big,
and it was tough for us to walk across it.
She had galoshes on and felt boots,
I had a pair of second-hand boots.
We forded streams and tramped across the forest;

each of my feet at every step it took
taking a smaller step inside the boot.
The child was feeble, I was certain of it.
"Boo-hoo," she'd say. "I'm tired," she'd say.
She'd tire in no time I was certain of it,
but as things turned out it was me who tired.
I growled I wasn't going any further
and sat down suddenly beside the fence.
"What's the matter with you?" she said.
"Don't be stupid! Put grass in your boots.
Do you want to eat something? Why won't you talk?
Hold this tin, this is crab.
We'll have refreshments. You small boys,
you're always pretending to be brave."
Then out I went across the prickly stubble
marching beside her in a few minutes.
Masculine pride was muttering in my mind:
I scraped together strength and I held out
for fear of what she'd say. I even whistled.
Grass was sticking out from my tattered boots.
So on and on
we walked without thinking of rest
passing craters, passing fires,
under the rocking sky of '41
tottering crazy on its smoking columns.

Y. YEVTUSHENKO

"More Light! More Light!"

Composed in the Tower before his execution
These moving verses, and being brought at that time
Painfully to the stake, submitted, declaring thus:
"I implore my God to witness that I have made no crime."

Nor was he forsaken of courage, but the death was horrible,
The sack of gunpowder failing to ignite.
His legs were blistered sticks on which the black sap
Bubbled and burst as he howled for the Kindly Light.

And that was but one, and by no means one of the worst;
Permitted at least his pitiful dignity;
And such as were by made prayers in the name of Christ,
That shall judge all men, for his soul's tranquillity.

We move now to outside a German wood.
Three men are there commanded to dig a hole
In which the two Jews are ordered to lie down
And be buried alive by the third, who is a Pole.

Not light from the shrine at Weimar beyond the hill
Nor light from heaven appeared. But he did refuse.
A Lüger settled back deeply in its glove.
He was ordered to change places with the Jews.

Much casual death had drained away their souls.
The thick dirt mounted toward the quivering chin.
When only the head was exposed the order came
To dig him out again and to get back in.

No light, no light in the blue Polish eye.
When he finished a riding boot packed down the earth.
The Lüger hovered lightly in its glove.
He was shot in the belly and in three hours bled to death.

No prayers or incense rose up in those hours
Which grew to be years, and every day came mute
Thousands sifting down through the crisp air
And settled upon his eyes in a black soot.

ANTHONY HECHT

Naming of Parts

Today we have naming of parts. Yesterday,
We had daily cleaning. And tomorrow morning
We shall have what to do after firing. But today,
To-day we have naming of parts. Japonica
Glistens like coral in all of the neighbouring gardens,
    And to-day we have naming of parts.

This is the lower sling swivel. And this
Is the upper sling swivel, whose use you will see,
When you are given your slings. And this is the piling swivel,
Which in your case you have not got. The branches
Hold in the gardens their silent, eloquent gestures,
    Which in our case we have not got.

This is the safety-catch, which is always released
With an easy flick of the thumb. And please do not let me
See anyone using his finger. You can do it quite easy
If you have any strength in your thumb. The blossoms
Are fragile and motionless, never letting anyone see
    Any of them using their finger.

And this you can see is the bolt. The purpose of this
Is to open the breech, as you see. We can slide it
Rapidly backwards and forwards: we call this
Easing the spring. And rapidly backwards and forwards
The early bees are assaulting and fumbling the flowers;
    They call it easing the Spring.

They call it easing the Spring: it is perfectly easy
If you have any strength in your thumb: like the bolt,
And the breech, and the cocking-piece, and the point of balance,

Which in our case we have not got; and the almond-blossom
Silent in all of the gardens and the bees going backwards and
    forwards,
    For today we have naming of parts.

HENRY REED

The Chances

I mind as 'ow the night afore that show
Us five got talking,—we was in the know—
"Over the top to-morrer; boys, we're for it.
First wave we are, first ruddy wave; that's tore it."
"Ah well," says Jimmy,—an' 'e's seen some scrappin'—
"There ain't more nor five things as can 'appen;—
Ye get knocked out; else wounded—bad or cushy;
Scuppered; or nowt except yer feeling mushy."

One of us got the knock-out, blown to chops.
T'other was hurt like, losin' both 'is props.
An' one, to use the word of 'ypocrites,
'Ad the misfortoon to be took be Fritz.
Now me, I wasn't scratched, praise God Almighty
(Though next time please I'll thank 'im for a blighty),
But poor young Jim, 'e's livin' an' 'e's not;
'E reckoned 'e'd five chances, an' 'e 'ad;
'E's wounded, killed, and pris'ner, all the lot,
The bloody lot all rolled in one. Jim's mad.

WILFRED OWEN

Vergissmeinicht

Three weeks gone and the combatants gone,
returning over the nightmare ground
we found the place again, and found
the soldier sprawling in the sun.

The frowning barrel of his gun
overshadowing. As we came on
that day, he hit my tank with one
like the entry of a demon.

Look. Here in the gunpit spoil
the dishonoured picture of his girl
who has put: "Steffi. Vergissmeinicht"
in a copybook gothic script.

We see him almost with content
abased, and seeming to have paid
and mocked at by his own equipment
that's hard and good when he's decayed.

But she would weep to see to-day
how on his skin the swart flies move;
the dust upon the paper eye
and the burst stomach like a cave.

For here the lover and killer are mingled
who had one body and one heart.
And death who had the soldier singled
has done the lover mortal hurt.

Homs, Tripolitania, 1943

KEITH DOUGLAS

Roman Wall Blues

Over the heather the wet wind blows,
I've lice in my tunic and a cold in my nose.

The rain comes pattering out of the sky,
I'm a Wall soldier, I don't know why.

The mist creeps over the hard grey stone,
My girl's in Tungria; I sleep alone.

Aulus goes hanging around her place,
I don't like his manners, I don't like his face.

Piso's a Christian, he worships a fish;
There'd be no kissing if he had his wish.

She gave me a ring but I diced it away;
I want my girl and I want my pay.

When I'm a veteran with only one eye
I shall do nothing but look at the sky.

W. H. AUDEN

Channel Firing

That night your great guns, unawares,
Shook all our coffins as we lay,
And broke the chancel window-squares,
We thought it was the Judgement-day

And sat upright. While drearisome
Arose the howl of wakened hounds:
The mouse let fall the altar-crumb,
The worms drew back into the mounds.

The glebe cow drooled. Till God called, "No";
It's gunnery practice out at sea
Just as before you went below;
The world is as it used to be:

"All nations striving strong to make
Red war yet redder. Mad as hatters
They do no more for Christés sake
Than you who are helpless in such matters.

"That this is not the judgement-hour
For some of them's a blessed thing,
For if it were they'd have to scour
Hell's floor for so much threatening . . .

"Ha, ha. It will be warmer when
I blow the trumpet (if indeed
I ever do; for you are men,
And rest eternal sorely need)".

So down we lay again. "I wonder,
Will the world ever saner be",
Said one, "than when He sent us under
in our indifferent century!"

And many a skeleton shook his head.
"Instead of preaching forty year",
My neighbour Parson Thirdly said,
"I wish I had stuck to pipes and beer."

Again the guns disturbed the hour,
Roaring their readiness to avenge,
As far inland as Stourton Tower,
And Camelot, and starlit Stonehenge.

THOMAS HARDY

Death of an Aircraft

(An incident of the Cretan campaign, 1941)
(to George Psychoundakis)

One day on our village in the month of July
An aeroplane sank from the sea of the sky,
    White as a whale it smashed on the shore
    Bleeding oil and petrol all over the floor.

The Germans advanced in the vertical heat
To save the dead plane from the people of Crete.
    And round the glass wreck in a circus of snow
    Set seven mechanical sentries to go.

Seven stalking spiders about the sharp sun
Clicking like clockwork and each with a gun.
    But at "Come to the Cookhouse" they wheeled about
    And sat down to sausages and sauerkraut.

Down from the mountain burning so brown
Wriggled three heroes from Kastelo town,
    Deep in the sand they silently sank
    And each struck a match for a petrol-tank.

Up went the plane in a feather of fire
As the bubbling boys began to retire
    And, grey in the guardhouse, seven Berliners
    Lost their stripes as well as their dinners.

Down in the village, at murder-stations,
The Germans fell in friends and relations:
    But not a Kastelian snapped an eye
    As he spat in the air and prepared to die.

Not a Kastelian whispered a word
Dressed with the dust to be massacred,
    And squinted up at the sky with a frown
    As three bubbly boys came walking down.

One was sent to the county gaol
Too young for bullets if not for bail,
    But the other two were in prime condition
    To take on a load of ammunition.

In Archontiki they stood in the weather
Naked, hungry, chained together:
    Stark as the stones in the market-place,
    Under the eyes of the populace.

Their irons unlocked as their naked hearts
They faced the squad and their funeral carts.
    The Captain cried, "Before you're away
    Is there any last word you'd like to say?"

"I want no words," said one, "with my lead,
Only some water to cool my head."
    "Water," the other said, "'s all very fine
    But I'll be taking a glass of wine.

A glass of wine for the afternoon
With permission to sing a signature-tune!"
    And he ran the *raki* down his throat
    And took a deep breath for the leading note.

But before the squad could shoot or say
Like the impala he leapt away
    Over the rifles, under the biers,
    The bullets rattling round his ears.

"Run!" they cried to the boy of stone
Who now stood there in the street alone,
    But, "Rather than bring revenge on your head
    It's better for me to die," he said.

The soldiers turned their machine-guns round
And shot him down with a dreadful sound
    Scrubbed his face with perpetual dark
    And rubbed it out like a pencil mark.

But his comrade slept in the olive tree
And sailed by night on the gnawing sea,
    The soldier's silver shilling earned
    And, armed like an archangel, returned.

CHARLES CAUSLEY

The Long War

Less passionate the long war throws
its burning thorn about all men,
caught in one grief, we share one wound,
and cry one dialect of pain.

We have forgot who fired the house,
whose easy mischief spilt first blood,
under one raging roof we lie
the fault no longer understood.

But as our twisted arms embrace
the desert where our cities stood,
death's family likeness in each face
must show, at last, our brotherhood.

LAURIE LEE

SECTION 5

In Town and Country

Preludes

I

The winter evening settles down
With smells of steaks in passageways.
Six o'clock.
The burnt-out ends of smoky days.
And now a gusty shower wraps
The grimy scraps
Of withered leaves about your feet
And newspapers from vacant lots;
The showers beat
On broken blinds and chimney-pots,
And at the corner of the street
A lonely cab-horse steams and stamps.
And then the lighting of the lamps.

II

The morning comes to consciousness
Of faint stale smells of beer
From the sawdust-trampled street
With all its muddy feet that press
To early coffee-stands.
With the other masquerades
That time resumes,
One thinks of all the hands
That are raising dingy shades
In a thousand furnished rooms.

T. S. ELIOT

The Early Purges

I was six when I first saw kittens drown.
Dan Taggart pitched them, "the scraggy wee shits",
Into a bucket; a frail metal sound,

Soft paws scraping like mad. But their tiny din
Was soon soused. They were slung on the snout
Of the pump and the water pumped in.

"Sure isn't it better for them now?" Dan said.
Like wet gloves they bobbed and shone till he sluiced
Them out on the dunghill, glossy and dead.

Suddenly frightened, for days I sadly hung
Round the yard, watching the three sogged remains
Turn mealy and crisp as old summer dung

Until I forgot them. But the fear came back
When Dan trapped big rats, snared rabbits, shot crows
Or, with a sickening tug, pulled old hens' necks.

Still, living displaces false sentiments
And now, when shrill pups are prodded to drown
I just shrug, "Bloody pups". It makes sense:

"Prevention of cruelty" talk cuts ice in town
Where they consider death unnatural,
But on well-run farms pests have to be kept down.

SEAMUS HEANEY

Winter-piece

You wake, all windows blind—embattled sprays
grained on the medieval glass.
Gates snap like gunshot
as you handle them. Five-barred fragility
sets flying fifteen rooks who go together
silently ravenous above this winter-piece
that will not feed them. They alight
beyond, scavenging, missing everything
but the bladed atmosphere, the white resistance.
Ruts with iron flanges track
through a hard decay
where you discern once more
oak-leaf by hawthorn, for the frost
rewhets their edges. In a perfect web
blanched along each spoke
and circle of its woven wheel,
the spider hangs, grasp unbroken
and death-masked in cold. Returning
you see the house glint-out behind
its holed and ragged glaze,
frost-fronds all streaming.

CHARLES TOMLINSON

Bank Holiday

Bright eyes in a pile of lumber
watching the spanking miles unroll
a seaside day in easy summer
    enter running or not at all
to the bodies without number
whoop of children swoop of gulls
    A lively tune on a tin whistle.

Blazing noon on a metal tangle
see the fat lady's skeleton mate,
Come and Get It, I'm No Angel,
    Kiss Me Quick Before It's Too Late;
Oh the bright and battering sandal
on the concrete's waste of heat
    Enter running or not at all.

Sandy mythologies by the mister
dribble nose and fly blown loose,
flags' and hands' heroic gestures;
    an old hat filling with booze
while the roaring roller coaster
flees its maze above the nudes
    Kiss me quick before it's too late.

Candy floss sticks, syrup waffles,
secret rides in the River Caves,
Scenes of the Harem, Sights Unlawful;
    widows and hucksters thick as thieves
and the day tilts at the bottle
and the starstruck girls believe.
    An old hat filling with booze.

Take me an air trip round the Tower
where, all glorious within,
spangles of the dancing floor
   shake a big bellyful of din
and balloons in splendid shower
fall to zips and hearts undone
   Widows and hucksters thick as thieves.

Rotherham Stockport Salford Nelson
Sheffield Burnley Bradford Shaw
roll by a shining Cinderella
   into the night's enormous maw,
smashin girl and luvly fella
tip the wink and close the door.
   Shake a big bellyful of din.

Sodden straws and french letters,
trodden ices, orange hulls,
clotted beach and crowded gutters,
   A lively tune on a tin whistle
sing to the sea "What matters . . . matters"
and the street sweepers and the gulls,
   Into night's enormous maw.

TONY CONNOR

Wind

This house has been far out at sea all night,
The woods crashing through darkness, the booming hills,
Winds stampeding the fields under the window
Floundering black astride and blinding wet

Till day rose; then under an orange sky
The hills had new places, and wind wielded
Blade-light, luminous black and emerald,
Flexing like the lens of a mad eye.

At noon I scaled along the house-side as far as
The coal-house door. I dared once to look up—
Through the brunt wind that dented the balls of my eyes
The tent of the hills drummed and strained its guyrope,

The fields quivering, the skyline a grimace,
At any second to bang and vanish with a flap:
The wind flung a magpie away and a black-
Back gull bent like an iron bar slowly. The house

Rang like some fine green goblet in the note
That any second would shatter it. Now deep
In chairs, in front of the great fire, we grip
Our hearts and cannot entertain book, thought,

Or each other. We watch the fire blazing,
And feel the roots of the house move, but sit on,
Seeing the window tremble to come in,
Hearing the stones cry out under the horizons.

TED HUGHES

Travelling Through the Dark

Travelling through the dark I found a deer
dead on the edge of the Wilson River road.
It is usually best to roll them into the canyon:
that road is narrow; to swerve might make more dead.

By glow of the tail-light I stumbled back of the car
and stood by the heap, a doe, a recent killing;
she had stiffened already, almost cold.
I dragged her off; she was large in the belly.

My fingers touching her side brought me the reason—
her side was warm; her fawn lay there waiting,
alive, still, never to be born.
Beside that mountain road I hesitated.

The car aimed ahead its lowered parking lights;
under the hood purred the steady engine.
I stood in the glare of the warm exhaust turning red;
around our group I could hear the wilderness listen.

I thought hard for us all—my only swerving—
then pushed her over the edge into the river.

WILLIAM STAFFORD

South Wales Mining Valley

Appearance is not reality.
For the illusion, stand
On this threadbare hillside
As it leans over its valley
In a miner's crouch, and
Trace deception in the
Patterned floor. The town
Borrows strength from its
Geometry, iterated in clean
Parallels of terraced rows
That stride the slopes, while
Pit-wheels, slag-cones, and
The ordered perpendiculars of
Stacks shape to a semblance of
Virility. Here, distance and
The grace of symmetry lend
An apparent power.
                              Descend now

To the streets and the
Formal figures break,
Become jagged, their edges
Being blurred by years of
Coal-dust. The houses stoop
The roads like shabby
Pensioners, and rust cramps
Winding-wheels. Once erect,
Chimneys, hollow now of
Smoke, fall into impotence.
Fading labourer! Energy
Should dominate but palsy
Grips, for where remoteness
Gave a purpose,
Contact shows a lie.

ALAN CRANG

January

The fox drags its wounded belly
Over the snow, the crimson seeds
Of blood burst with a mild explosion,
Soft as excrement, bold as roses.

Over the snow that feels no pity,
Whose white hands can give no healing,
The fox drags its wounded belly.

R. S. THOMAS

The Jaguar

The apes yawn and adore their fleas in the sun.
The parrots shriek as if they were on fire, or strut
Like cheap tarts to attract the stroller with the nut.
Fatigued with indolence, tiger and lion

Lie still as the sun. The boa-constrictor's coil
Is a fossil. Cage after cage seems empty, or
Stinks of sleepers from the breathing straw.
It might be painted on a nursery wall.

But who runs like the rest past these arrives
At a cage where the crowd stands, stares, mesmerized,
As a child at a dream, at a jaguar hurrying enraged
Through prison darkness after the drills of his eyes

On a short fierce fuse, Not in boredom—
The eye satisfied to be blind in fire,
By the bang of blood in the brain deaf the ear—
He spins from the bars, but there's no cage to him

More than to the visionary in his cell:
His stride is wildernesses of freedom:
The world rolls under the long thrust of his heel.
Over the cage floor the horizons come.

TED HUGHES

Sheep Gathering

What impresses in this scene of gathering
is its purpose.
We break our climb, pleased to watch
the comforting liaison
between man and beast
against this brooding background—
dogs responding to whistles,
wheeling over wayward rocks
in circles of confidence,
sweeping into patterns
the litter of haphazard dots.

Across the valley
we see the scene repeat itself
in long shot,
with white columns
sliding like mercury off bald slopes
to a single blob.

Such assurance brings its own relief,
blunting the mountains harshness.
Glad to endow these dogs with intellect,
we admire the way they round
with sergeant-major-like allegiance
these threadbare legions,
their discipline imposing order
where caprice would dominate.

ALAN CRANG

The Proper Due

A thin willow hovers here:
Lovely—lovely in spite of
  The thick drain oozing near
Between sick banks, a vein of evil.

  Lovely because of . . .
For acres of willows look like nothing.
  Beauty defines itself against the dirt,
That telling reflection—
  Like health against a hurt—
Deep in the dark infection.

  Hell is easy to foretell—
Mud without the willow,
  Shallow silence with not a single bell,
Still shadow of exhausted monologue.

  Hard to envisage Heaven—
Acres of willows, haloes in eternal floodlights,
  Ten thousand harps that keep in time?
Our best imagination: sights,
  Free and frequent, of the distant slime.

  So one returns to earth, to see again
The willow, and to pay the filth its proper due.
  That in the end—the very end—one vision
Grows from two.

                    D. J. Enright

The Unknown Citizen

(To JS/07/M/378
This Marble Monument
Is Erected by the State)

He was found by the Bureau of Statistics to be
One against whom there was no official complaint,
And all the reports on his conduct agree
That, in the modern sense of an old-fashioned word, he was a saint,
For in everything he did he served the Greater Community.
Except for the War till the day he retired
He worked in a factory and never got fired,
But satisfied his employers, Fudge Motors Inc.
Yet he wasn't a scab or odd in his views,
For his Union reports that he paid his dues,
(Our report on his Union shows it was sound)
And our Social Psychology workers found
That he was popular with his mates and liked a drink.
The Press are convinced that he bought a paper every day
And that his reactions to advertisements were normal in every way.
Policies taken out in his name prove that he was fully insured,
And his Health-card shows that he was once in hospital but left it
        cured.
Both Producers Research and High-Grade Living declare
He was fully sensible to the advantages of the Instalment Plan
And had everything necessary to the Modern Man,
A phonograph, a radio, a car and a frigidaire.
Our researchers into Public Opinion are content
That he held the proper opinions for the time of the year;
When there was peace, he was for peace; when there was war, he
        went.
He was married and added five children to the population,
Which our Eugenist says was the right number for a parent of his
        generation,

And our teachers report that he never interfered with their
    education.
Was he free? Was he happy? The question is absurd:
Had anything been wrong, we should certainly have heard.

W. H. AUDEN

SECTION 6

Against the Law

Jesse James

It was on a Wednesday night, the moon was shining bright,
   They robbed the Danville train.
And the people they did say, for many miles away,
   'Twas the outlaws Frank and Jesse James.

Jesse had a wife to mourn him all her life,
   The children they are brave.
'Twas a dirty little coward shot Mister Howard,
   And laid Jesse James in his grave.
(Chorus to be repeated after each verse.)

Jesse was a man was a friend to the poor,
   He never left a friend in pain.
And with his brother Frank he robbed Chicago bank
   And then held up the Glendale train.

It was Robert Ford, the dirty little coward,
   I wonder how he does feel,
For he ate of Jesse's bread and he slept in Jesse's bed,
   Then he laid Jesse James in his grave.

It was his brother Frank that robbed Gallatin bank,
   And carried the money from the town.
It was in this very place that they had a little race,
   For they shot Captain Sheets to the ground.

They went to the crossing not very far from there,
   And there they did the same;
And the agent on his knees he delivered up the keys
   To the outlaws Frank and Jesse James.

It was on a Saturday night, Jesse was at home
  Talking to his family brave,
When the thief and the coward, little Robert Ford,
  Laid Jesse James in his grave.

How the people held their breath when they heard of Jesse's
    death,
  And wondered how he ever came to die.
'Twas one of the gang, dirty Robert Ford,
  That shot Jesse James on the sly.

Jesse went to rest with his hands on his breast;
  He died with a smile on his face.
He was born one day in the county of Clay,
  And came from a solitary race.

ANONYMOUS

Nile Fishermen

Naked men, fishing in Nile without a licence,
kneedeep in it, pulling gaunt at stretched ropes.
Round the next bend is the police boat and the officials
ready to make an arrest on the yellow sand.

The splendid bodies are stark to the swimming sand,
taut to the ruffled water, the flickering palms,
yet swelling and quivering as they tug at the trembling ropes.
Their faces are bent along the arms and still.

Sun is torn in coloured petals on the water,
the water shivering in the heat and the north wind;
and near and far billow out white swollen crescents,
the clipping wings of feluccas, seagull sails.

A plunge in the turbid water, a quick joke stirs
a flashing of teeth, an invocation of God.
Here is food to be fetched and living from labour.
The tight ropes strain and the glittering backs for the haul.

Round the bend comes the police boat. The men scatter.
The officials blow their whistles on the golden sand.
They overtake and arrest strong bodies of men
who follow with sullen faces, and leave their nets behind.

REX WARNER

Johnie Armstrong

There dwelt a man in faire Westmerland,
    Johnie Armstrong men did him call,
He had nither lands nor rents coming in,
    Yet he kept eight score men in his hall.

He had horse and harness for them all,
    Goodly steeds were all milke-white;
O the golden bands an about their necks,
    And their weapons, they were all alike.

Newes then was brought unto the king
    That there was such a won as hee,
That lived lyke a bold out-law,
    And robbed all the north country.

The king he writt an a letter then,
    A letter which was large and long;
He signed it with his owner hand;
    And he promised to doe him no wrong.

When this letter came Johnie unto,
   His heart was as blythe as birds on the tree:
"Never was I sent for before any king,
   My father, my grandfather, nor none but mee.

"And if wee goe the king before,
   I would we went most orderly;
Every man of you shall have his scarlet cloak,
   Laced with silver laces three.

"Every won of you shall have his velvett coat,
   Laced with silver lace so white;
O the golden bands an about your necks,
   Black hatts, white feathers, all alyke."

By the morrow morninge at ten of the clock,
   Towards Edenburough gon was hee,
And with him all his eight score men;
   Good Lord, it was a goodly sight for to see!

When Johnie came befower the king,
   He fell downe on his knee;
"O pardon, my soveraine leige," he said,
   "O pardon my eight score men and mee!"

"Thou shalt have no pardon, thou traytor strong,
   For thy eight score men nor thee;
For tomorrow morning by ten of the clock,
   Both thou and them shall hang on the gallow-tree."

But Johnie look'd over his left shoulder,
   Good Lord, what a grievous look looked hee!
Saying, "Asking grace of a graceles face—
   Why there is none for you nor me."

But Johnie had a bright sword by his side,
  And it was made of the mettle so free,
That had not the king stept his foot aside,
  He had smitten his head from his faire bodde.

Saying, "Fight on, my merry men all,
  And see that none of you be taine;
For rather then men shall we say were hange'd,
  Let them report how we were slaine."

Then, God wott, faire Eddenburrough rose,
  And so besett poore Johnie rounde,
That fowerscore and tenn of Johnie's best men
  Lay gasping all upon the ground.

Then like a mad man Johnie laid about,
  And like a mad man then fought hee,
Untill a falce Scot came Johnie behinde,
  And runn him through the fair boddee.

Saying, "Fight on, my merry men all,
  And see that none of you be taine;
For I will stand by and bleed but awhile,
  And then will I come and fight againe."

Newes then was brought to young Johnie Armstrong,
  As he stood by his nurse's knee,
Who vowed if ere he lived for to be a man,
  On the treacherous Scots revenged hee'd be.

ANONYMOUS

A Rope for Harry Fat

"Te Whiu was a Maori lad in his late teens who was hanged for killing an old lady. It seems that she surprised him when he was burgling her house, and he killed her in panic. He said that he needed the money to buy a bicycle. He was perhaps a bit simple. ... —I was angry about this hanging of a boy and ... —tried to prevent it."

JAMES BAXTER

Oh some have killed in angry love
    And some have killed in hate,
And some have killed in foreign lands
    To serve the business State.
The hangman's hands are abstract hands
    Though sudden death they bring—
"The hangman keeps our country pure,"
    Says Harry Fat the King.

Young love will kick the chairs about
    And like a rush fire burn,
Desiring what it cannot have,
    A true love in return.
Who knows what rage and darkness fall
    When lovers' thoughts grow cold?
"Whoever kills must pay the price,"
    Says Harry Fat the Old.

With violent hands a young man tries
    To mend the shape of life.
This one used a shotgun
    And that one used a knife.
And who can see the issues plain
    That rack our groaning dust?
"The law is greater than the man,"
    Says Harry Fat the Just.

Te Whiu was too young to vote
  The prison records show:
Some thought he was too young to hang.
  Legality said No.
Who knows what fear the raupo hides
  Or where the wild duck flies?
"A trapdoor and a rope is best,"
  Says Harry Fat the Wise.

Though many a time he rolled his coat
  And on the bare boards lay,
He lies in heavy concrete now
  Until The Reckoning Day.
In linen sheet or granite aisle
  Sleep Ministers of State.
"We cannot help the idle poor,"
  Says Harry Fat the Great.

Mercy stirred like a summer wind
  The wigs and polished boots
And the long Jehovah faces
  Above their Sunday suits.
The jury was uncertain,
  The judge debated long;
"Let Justice take her rightful course,"
  Said Harry Fat the Strong.

The butcher boy and baker boy
  Were whistling in the street
When the hangman bound Te Whiu's eyes
  And strapped his hands and feet,
Who stole to buy a bicycle
  And killed in panic blood.
"The parson won his soul at length,"
  Said Harry Fat the Good.

Oh some will kill in rage and fear
  And some will kill in hate,
And some will kill in foreign lands
  To serve the master State.
Justice walks heavy in the land
  She bears a rope and shroud.
"We will not change our policy,"
  Says Harry Fat the Proud.

JAMES BAXTER

The Burglary

It's two o'clock now; somebody's pausing in the street
to turn up his collar. The night's black: distraught
with chimney-toppling wind and harsh rain—
see, the wet's soaking in on the end-gable,
and the frothing torrent, overspilling the broken drain,

accosts the pavement with incoherent babble.
There is the house we want: how easy to burgle,
with its dark trees, and the lawn set back from the road;
the owners will be in bed now—the old couple;
you've got the position of the safe?—Yes, I know the code.

The cock's going mad up there on the church steeple;
the wind's enormous—will it ever stifle;
still, its noise, and the rain's are with us, I daresay,
they'll cover what we make, if we go careful
round by the greenhouse, and in at the back way.

Here's the broken sash I mentioned;—no need to be
    fearful,
watch how I do it: these fingers are facile
with the practice I've had on worse nights than this.
I tell you, the whole thing's going to be a doddle:
the way I've got it worked out, we can't miss.

Although, God knows, most things turn out a muddle,
and it only confuses more to look for a moral.
Wherever I've been the wind and rain's blown;—
I've done my best to hang on, as they tried to whittle
the name from the action, the flesh away from the bone,

but I think, sometimes, I'm fighting a losing battle.
So many bad nights; so many strange homes to burgle;
and every job done with a mate I don't know:—
oh, you're all right; I don't mean to be personal,
but when the day breaks, you'll have your orders, and go.

Then, the next time the foul weather howls in the ginnel;
when the slates slide, the brimming gutters gurgle;
there'll be another lad I've never seen before,
with the rest of the knowledge that makes the job possible
as I ease up a window or skeleton-key a door.

Still, it's my only life, and I've no quarrel
with the boss's methods;—apart from the odd quibble
about allowances and fair rates of pay,
or the difficult routes I often have to travel,
or the fact that I never get a holiday.

Most of the time, though, I'm glad of mere survival,
even at the stormiest hour of the darkest vigil.
. . . Here's the hall door; under the stairs, you said?
This one's easy, because the old folk are feeble,
and lie in their curtained room, sleeping like the dead.

Sometimes, believe me, it's a lot more trouble,
when you've got to be silent, and move as though through
    treacle.
Now hold your breath while I let these tumblers click . . .
I've done these many a time . . . a well known model;
one more turn now . . . Yes; that does the trick.

Nothing inside? The same recurrent muddle;
I think the most careful plan's a bloody marvel
if it plays you true, if nothing at all goes wrong.
Well, let's be off; we've another place to tackle
under the blown, black, rain; and the dawn won't be long

when the wind will drop, and the rain become a drizzle,
and you'll go your way. Leaving me the bedraggled
remnants of night, that walk within the head
long after the sun-shot gutters cease to trickle,
and I draw my curtains, and topple into bed.

TONY CONNOR

My Friend Maloney

My friend Maloney, eighteen,
  Swears like a sentry,
Got into trouble two years back
  With the local gentry.

Parson and squire's sons
  Informed a copper.
The magistrates took one look at Maloney.
  Fixed him proper.

Talked of the crime of youth,
  The innocent victim.
Maloney never said a blind word
  To contradict him.

Maloney of Gun Street,
  Back of the Nuclear Mission,
Son of the town whore,
  Blamed television.

Justice, as usual, triumphed.
  Everyone felt fine.
Things went deader.
  Maloney went up the line.

Maloney learned one lesson:
  Never play the fool
With the products of especially a minor
  Public school.

Maloney lost a thing or two
  At that institution.

First shirt, second innocence,
  The old irresolution.

Found himself a girl-friend,
  Sharp suit, sharp collars.
Maloney on a moped,
  Pants full of dollars.

College boys on the corner
  In striped, strait blazers
Look at old Maloney,
  Eyes like razors.

You don't need talent, says Maloney.
   You don't need looks,
All I got you got, fellers.
   You can keep your thick books.

Parson got religion,
   Squire, in the end, the same.
The magistrate went over the wall.
   Life, said Maloney, 's a game.

Consider then the case of Maloney,
   College boys, parson, squire, beak.
Who was the victor and who was the victim?
   Speak.

CHARLES CAUSLEY

The Poacher

Turning aside, never meeting
In the still lanes, fly infested,
Our frank greeting with quick smile,
You are the wind that set the bramble
Aimlessly clawing the void air.
The fox knows you, the sly weasel
Feels always the steel comb
Of eyes parting like sharp rain
Among the grasses its smooth fur.
No smoke haunting the cold chimney
Over your hearth betrays your dwelling
In blue writing above the trees.
The robed night, your dark familiar,
Covers your movements; the slick sun,
A dawn accomplice, removes your tracks
One by one from the bright dew.

R. S. THOMAS

The Fair

Music and yellow steam, the fizz
Of spinning lights as roundabouts
Galloping nowhere whirl and whizz
Through fusillades of squeals and shouts;
The night sniffs rich at pungent spice,
Brandysnap and diesel oil;
The stars like scattered beads of rice
Sparsely fleck the sky's deep soil
Dulled and diminished by these trapped
Melodic meteors below
In whose feigned fever brightly lapped
The innocent excitements flow.
Pocketfuls of simple thrills
Jingle silver, purchasing
A warm and sugared fear that spills
From dizzy car and breathless swing.
So no one hears the honest shriek
From the field beyond the fair,
A single voice becoming weak,
Then dying on the ignorant air.
And not for hours will frightened love
Rise and seek her everywhere,
Then find her, like a fallen glove,
Soiled and crumpled, lying there.

VERNON SCANNELL

What's the Difference?

The world (one often hears)
Must be full of murderers.
Not all that many are caught;
There are plenty walking about.

Sometimes they pull it off
And lead a blameless life,
Good to the wives they wed
By bashing in someone's head.

So it's natural to wonder how
They differ from me or you.
Conscience? Consciences are
As calm as they appear.

I can make out in the sea
That washes my memory
Storms as sombre as ever
Darkened to wicked weather;

Hatred so great it might
Press my fingers as tight
On windpipe or on gun
As now around this pen.

If conscience is a sea
It answers from day to day
To what the weather is like.
The rest is only luck.

Did your girl say no
When the storm began to blow?
Was somebody passing when
You happened to raise the gun?

Weather's another name
For imagination;
And if yours is blustery
It imposes on the sea

Billows that rear up higher
Than intention, even desire;
Or a slow enormous swell
That is more than enough to kill.

LAURENCE LERNER

SECTION 7

Crabbed Age and Youth

In Just Spring

in Just—
spring   when the world is mud—
luscious the little
lame balloonman

whistles   far   and wee

and eddieandbill come
running from marbles and
piracies and it's
spring

when the world is puddle-wonderful

the queer
old balloonman whistles
far   and   wee
and bettyandisbel come dancing

from hop-scotch and jump-rope and

it's
spring
and
    the

        goat-footed

balloonMan   whistles
far
and
wee

                    E. E. CUMMINGS

Navaho Children,
Canyon de Chelly, Arizona

You sprouted from the sand,
running, stopping, running;
beyond you tall red
tons of rock rested
on the feathery tamarisk.

Torn jeans, T-shirts
lope and skip, toes drum
and you're coming
full tilt
for the lollipops,

hopefully
arrive, daren't
look, for our stares
(your noses dribble)
prove too rude

in your silence,
can't break, either,
your upturned
monkey faces into smiles.
It's no joke

as you grope
up, up
to the driver's door, take
them reverently, the
lollipops—

your smallest, too small,
waited three
paces back, shuffling,
then provided,
evidently

by a sister on tiptoe who
takes his hand, helps
unwrap the sugar totem.
And we are swept
on, bouncing,

look back,
seeing walls
dwarf you. But how
could you get any
more thin, small, far.

CHRISTOPHER MIDDLETON

Hunting with a Stick

Once, ten years old, in the cobweb sun
I chased a rabbit on stiffening grass
Till it twinkled into its hole of sand.
Although I knew that the hunt was done
(For rabbits burrow deeper than fire)
I crouched and crept there, stretching my hand,
And kneeling my shadow on frost I saw
In a turn of the hole too tight to pass
Its fluffed fat haunches were firmly jammed,
Its white tail sat as still as a star.

The moment froze in a single breath:
Give me a second and I could be quick,
Having spent ten years in the ways of death,
And I wanted this death, not one planned.
I thrust at its buttocks with my stick
And felt the soft bone go under the fur,
The silence I knelt on echo and stir,
The green meat of mornings that made me sick . . .

I dragged it back by a fistful of hair,
Then flourishing my prize with a dripping claw;
But dangling it upwards again I saw
Its face was bitten and muffled in blood,
One eye was empty and showed the skull,
The soft jaw was eaten into a snarl,
Death hung from its ears in a glistening hood.

And at ten years old I first understood
There were other deaths in the world than me,
More ways to kill than with stone and stick:
While my shadow falconed it from the air
A stoat had sat in its horror there
And bitten its burrowing bone to the quick.

MICHAEL BALDWIN

The Young Ones

They slip on to the bus, hair piled up high.
New styles each month, it seems to me. I look,
Not wanting to be seen, casting my eye
Above the unread pages of a book.

They are fifteen or so. When I was thus,
I huddled in school coats, my satchel hung
Lop-sided on my shoulder. Without fuss
These enter adolescence; being young

Seems good to them, a state we cannot reach,
No talk of "awkward ages" now. I see
How childish gazes staring out of each
Unfinished face prove me incredibly

Old-fashioned. Yet at least I have the chance
To size up several stages—young yet old,
Doing the twist, mocking an "old-time" dance:
So many ways to be unsure or bold.

ELIZABETH JENNINGS

Black Jackets

In the silence that prolongs the span
Rawly of music when the record ends,
    The red-haired boy who drove a van
In weekday overalls but, like his friends,

    Wore cycle boots and jacket here
To suit the Sunday hangout he was in,
    Heard, as he stretched back from his beer,
Leather creak softly round his neck and chin.

    Before him, on a coal-black sleeve
Remote exertion had lined, scratched, and burned
    Insignia that could not revive
The heroic fall or climb where they were earned.

On the other drinkers bent together,
Concocting selves for their impervious kit,
   He saw it as no more than leather
Which, taut across the shoulders grown to it,

   Sent through the dimness of a bar
As sudden and anonymous hints of light
   As those that shipping give, that are
Now flickers on the Bay, now lost in night.

   He stretched out like a cat, and rolled
The bitterish taste of beer upon his tongue,
   And listened to a joke being told:
The present was the things he stayed among.

   If it was only loss he wore,
He wore it to assert, with fierce devotion,
   Complicity and nothing more.
He recollected his initiation,

   And one especially of the rites.
For on his shoulders they had put tattoos:
   The group's name on the left, The Knights,
And on the right the slogan Born To Lose.

THOM GUNN

The Boys

Six of them climbed aboard,
None of them twenty yet,
At a station up the line:
Flannel shirts rimmed with sweat,
Boots bulled to outrageous shine,
Box-pleats stiff as a board.

Pinkly, smelling of Bass,
They lounged on the blue moquette
And rubbed their blanco off.
One told of where to get
The best crumpet. A cough
From the corner. One wrote on the glass

A word in common use.
The others stirred and jeered.
"Reveille" was idled through
Till the next station appeared,
And the six of them all threw
Their Weights on the floor. Excuse

For a laugh on the platform. Then
We rattled, and moved away,
The boys only just through the door.
It was near the end of the day.
Two slept. One farted and swore,
And went on about his women.

Three hours we had watched this lot,
All of us family men,
Responsible, set in our ways.
I looked at my paper again:
Another H-test. There are days
You wonder whether you're not

Out of touch, old hat, gone stale.
I remembered my twenty-first,
In the NAAFI, laid out cold.
Then one of them blew and burst
A bag; and one of the old
Told them to stow it. The pale

Lights of the city came near.
We drew in and stopped. The six
Bundled their kit and ran.
"A good belting would sort out their tricks",
Said my neighbour, a well-spoken man.
"Yes, but . . . " But he didn't hear.

ANTHONY THWAITE

Crabbed Age and Youth

Crabbed Age and Youth
Cannot live together:
Youth is full of pleasance,
Age is full of care;
Youth like summer morn,
Age like winter weather;
Youth like summer brave,
Age like winter bare.
Youth is full of sport,
Age's breath is short;
Youth is nimble, Age is lame;
Youth is hot and bold,
Age is weak, and cold;
Youth is wild, and Age is tame.
Age, I do abhor thee;
Youth, I do adore thee;
O, my Love, my Love is young!
Age, I do defy thee:
O, sweet shepherd, hie thee!
For methinks thou stay'st too long.

WILLIAM SHAKESPEARE?

The Hunchback in the Park

The hunchback in the park
A solitary mister
Propped between trees and water
From the opening of the garden lock
That lets the trees and water enter
Until the Sunday sombre bell at dark.

Eating bread from a newspaper
Drinking water from the chained cup
That the children filled with gravel
In the fountain basin where I sailed my ship
Slept at night in a dog kennel
But nobody chained him up.

Like the park birds he came early
Like the water he sat down
And Mister they called him Hey mister
The truant boys from the town
Running when he heard them clearly
On out of sound

Past lake and rockery
Laughing when he shook his paper
Hunchbacked in mockery
Through the loud zoo of the willow groves
Dodging the park keeper
With his stick that picked up leaves.

And the old dog sleeper
Alone between nurses and swans
While the boys among willows

Made the tigers jump out of their eyes
To roar on the rockery stones
And the groves were blue with sailors

Made all day until bell time
A woman figure without fault
Straight as a young elm
Straight and tall from his crooked bones
That she might stand in the night
After the locks and chains

All night in the unmade park
After the railings and shrubberies
The birds the grass the trees the lake
And the wild boys innocent as strawberries
Had followed the hunchback
To his kennel in the dark.

DYLAN THOMAS

Old Man Asleep

He takes the snuff-box from his pocket and,
As many times before, taps on the lid.
The day's newspaper slips on to the floor;
He does not notice now, so near to sleep.
    His chin falls on his chest.
He sleeps more in the daytime than at night.

He has antagonised so many people,
Argued with them and scoffed and cursed their views,
Few men or women come with pleasure now;
All are afraid, except his wife who must
    Have kept the image of
Him being gentle, does not see he's changed.

All meanings lie in fragments; explanations
Of motive—disappointment, love, revenge—
Are too far scattered to reveal a pattern.
Only his anger holds this man together
   And keeps him safe within
The little circle no one dares to cross.

He has loved once with hands and eyes but now
Both are like useless tools. His hands are cunning
Only with his small pleasures, will not stretch
In love or trust. He hates, yet wants, our pity,
   Having so little time
To find compassion for his own near death.

ELIZABETH JENNINGS

Eighty-one Years Old

She wants to die and all of us
Agree although we do not say;
Instead, we tend her every day,
Bring flowers and food without much fuss.
She stares at us and we stare back,
Each knowing what the others lack.

She cannot die. At times, her heart
Moves slowly, almost stops and then
The lingering life begins again,
New days of sickness have to start.
Someone must always be near by;
She must not be alone to die.

And that is what she longs for most—
To be alone, when no one stands
With filled but with unhelping hands.
Even the priest who brings the Host
Cannot provide the peace but stays
To join in mumbled words of praise.

An empty space, a dusted room—
These will be left when she at last
Becomes her own self-willed outcast.
And guilty thoughts, no doubt, will come
To nurses who had wished her dead
And now have nothingness instead.

ELIZABETH JENNINGS

SECTION 8

Love's Another Thing

The Picnic

It is the picnic with Ruth in the spring.
Ruth was third on my list of seven girls
But the first two were gone (Betty) or else
Had someone (Ellen had accepted Doug).
Indian Gully the last day of school;
Girls make the lunches for the boys too.
I wrote a note to Ruth in algebra class
Day before the test. She smiled, and nodded.
We left the cars and walked through the young corn
The shoots green as paint and the leaves like tongues
Trembling. Beyond the fence where we stood
Some wild strawberry flowered by an elm tree
And Jack-in-the-pulpit was olive ripe.
A blackbird fled as I crossed, and showed
A spot of gold or red under its quick wing.
I held the wire for Ruth and watched the whip
Of her long, striped skirt as she followed.
Three freckles blossomed on her thin, white back
Underneath the loop where the blouse buttoned.
We went for our lunch away from the rest,
Stretched in the new grass, our heads close
Over unknown things wrapped up in wax papers.
Ruth tried for the same, I forget what it was,
And our hands were together. She laughed,
And a breeze caught the edge of her little
Collar and the edge of her brown, loose hair
That touched my cheek. I turned my face into
The gentle fall. I saw how sweet it smelled.
She didn't move her head or take her hand.
I felt a soft caving in my stomach

As at the top of the highest slide
When I had been a child, but was not afraid,
And did not know why my eyes moved with wet
As I brushed her cheek with my lips and brushed
Her lips with my own lips. She said to me
Jack, Jack, different than I had ever heard,
Because she wasn't calling me, I think,
Or telling me. She used my name to
Talk in another way I wanted to know.
She laughed again and then she took her hand;
I gave her what we both had touched—can't
Remember what it was, and we ate the lunch.
Afterward we walked in the small, cool creek
Our shoes off, her skirt hitched, and she smiling,
My pants rolled, and then we climbed up the high
Side of Indian Gully and looked
Where we had been, our hands together again.
It was then some bright thing came in my eyes,
Starting at the back of them and flowing
Suddenly through my head and down my arms
And stomach and my bare legs that seemed not
To stop in feet, not to feel the red earth
Of the Gully, as though we hung in a
Touch of birds. There was a word in my throat
With the feeling and I knew the first time
What it meant and I said, it's beautiful.
Yes, she said, and I felt the sound and word
In my hand join the sound and word in hers
As in one name said, or in one cupped hand.
We put back on our shoes and socks and we
Sat in the grass awhile, crosslegged, under
A blowing tree, not saying anything.
And Ruth played with shells she found in the creek,
As I watched. Her small wrist which was so sweet
To me turned by her breast and the shells dropped
Green, white, blue, easily into her lap,

Passing light through themselves. She gave the pale
Shells to me, and got up and touched her hips
With her light hands, and we walked down slowly
To play the school games with the others.

JOHN LOGAN

Unholy Marriage

POLICE ARE SEEKING TO IDENTIFY THE
PILLION RIDER WHO WAS ALSO KILLED

Her mother bore her, father cared
And clothed her body, young and neat.
The careful virgin had not shared
Cool soft anointment of her breast
Or any other sweet,
But kept herself for best.

How sweet she would have been in bed,
Her bridegroom sighing in her hair,
His tenderness heaped on her head,
Receiving benediction from her breast
With every other fair
She kept for him, the best.

Who she is now they do not know
Assembling her body on a sheet.
This foolish virgin shared a blow
That drove her almost through a stranger's breast
And all her sweet
Mingles with his in dust.

Unwilling marriage, her blood runs with one
Who bought for a few pounds and pence
A steel machine able to "do a ton",
Not knowing at a ton a straw will pierce a breast:
No wheel has built-in sense,
Not yet the shiniest and best.

And so, "doing a ton", in fog and night
Before he could think, Christ! or she could moan
There came a heavy tail without a light
And many tons compressed each back to breast
And blood and brain and bone
Mixed, lay undressed.

Anointed only by the punctured oil
Poured like unleashed wind or fire from bag
Sold by some damned magician out to spoil
The life that girded in this young girl's breast
Now never to unfurl her flag
And march love's happy quest.

Her mother hears the clock; her father sighs,
Takes off his boots: she's late tonight.
I hope she's a careful virgin: men have eyes
For cherished daughters growing in the breast.
Some news? They hear the gate
A man comes: not the best.

DAVID HOLBROOK

If You'll Give Me a Kiss and Be My Girl

If you'll give me a kiss and be my girl
Jump on my bike, we'll do a ton.
We'll explode from the city in a cloud of dust
And roar due west to the setting sun.

We'll bounce the days all over the beach
Pop them like seaweed and scatter ourselves
Careless as kids with candy floss
Into all the shapes of all of the shells.

We'll go as giddy as merry-go-rounds
Bump with a crash like dodgem cars
Float in a basket of coloured balloons
Or jump in a rocket and whizz for Mars.

If you love to be blown by a roar of wind
If you love to twist and spin and twirl
If you love to crash on the shore like waves
Then give me a kiss and be my girl.

I love to be blown by a roar of wind
But I love to watch the sea asleep
And breathe in salt and fresh-caught shrimps
As we wind our way through snoring streets.

I'll jive in a cellar till the band drops dead
But I want you to sing on your own guitar
For no one but me and a moonlight oak
Then dive in the silent lake for a star.

I love to twist the night away
But I love to hold you dark and still.
I love your kick that drives us miles
But I love the view from the top of a hill.

But if you give me the crashing waves
And sing me the blues of the sea as well,
Then, whether there's candyfloss or not,
I'll give you a kiss and be your girl.

LEO AYLEN

The Fireman's Not for Me

Come all you young maidens, take warning from me,
    Shun all engine firemen and their company;
He'll tell you he loves you and all kinds of lies,
    But the one that he loves is the train that he drives.

I once loved a fireman and he said he loved me;
    He took me a-walking into the country;
He hugged me and kissed me and gazed in my eyes,
    And said, "You're as nice as the eight-fortyfive!"

He said, "My dear Molly, just say you'll be mine;
    Just give me the signal and let's clear the line.
My fires they are burning and the steam it is high—
    If you don't take the brakes off I think I will die."

I gave him this answer, saying, "Don't make so free!"
    For no loco fireman shall ever have me!
He'll take all your love and then, when you're in need,
    He races away at the top of his speed.

A sailor comes home when his voyage is done,
    A soldier gets weary of following the drum,
A collier will cleave to his loved one for life—
    But a fireman's one love is the engine, his wife!

EWAN MCCOLL

The Whitsun Weddings

That Whitsun, I was late getting away:
   Not till about
One-twenty on the sunlit Saturday
Did my three-quarters-empty train pull out,
All windows down, all cushions hot, all sense
Of being in a hurry gone. We ran
Behind the backs of houses, crossed a street
Of blinding windscreens, smelt the fish-dock; thence
The river's level drifting breadth began,
Where sky and Lincolnshire and water meet.

All afternoon, through the tall heat that slept
   For miles inland,
A slow and stopping curve southwards we kept.
Wide farms went by, short-shadowed cattle, and
Canals with floatings of industrial froth;
A hothouse flashed, uniquely; hedges dipped
And rose; and now and then a smell of grass
Displaced the reek of buttoned carriage-cloth
Until the next town, new and nondescript,
Approached with acres of dismantled cars.

At first, I didn't notice what a noise
   The weddings made
Each station that we stopped at: sun destroys
The interests of what's happening in the shade,
And down the long cool platforms whoops and skirls
I took for porters larking with the mails
And went on reading. Once we started, though,
We passed them, grinning and pomaded, girls
In parodies of fashion, heels and veils,
All posed irresolutely, watching us go,

As if out on the end of an event
   Waving goodbye
To something that survived it. Struck, I leant
More promptly out next time, more curiously,
And saw it all again in different terms:
The fathers with broad belts under their suits
And seamy foreheads; mothers loud and fat;
An uncle shouting smut; and then the perms,
The nylon gloves and jewellery-substitutes,
The lemons, mauves, and olive-ochres that

Marked off the girls unreally from the rest.
   Yes, from cafes
And banquet-halls up yards, and bunting-dressed
Coach-party annexes, the wedding-days
Were coming to an end. All down the line
Fresh couples climbed aboard; the rest stood round;
The last confetti and advice were thrown,
And, as we moved, each face seemed to define
Just what it saw departing: children frowned
At something dull; fathers had never known

Success so huge and wholly farcical;
   The women shared
The secret like a happy funeral;
While girls, gripping their handbags tighter, stared
At a religious wounding. Free at last,
And loaded with the sum of all they saw,
We hurried towards London, shuffling gouts of steam.
Now fields were building-plots, and poplars cast
Long shadows over major roads, and for
Some fifty minutes, that in time would seem

Just long enough to settle hats and say
   "I nearly died",
A dozen marriages got under way.

They watched the landscape, sitting side by side
—An Odeon went past, a cooling tower,
And someone running up to bowl—and none
Thought of the others they would never meet
Or how their lives would all contain this hour.
I thought of London spread out in the sun,
Its postal districts packed like squares of wheat:

There we were aimed. And as we raced across
   Bright knots of rails
Past standing Pullmans, walls of blackened moss
Came close, and it was nearly done, this frail
Travelling coincidence; and what it held
Stood ready to be loosed with all the power
That being changed can give. We slowed again,
And as the tightened brakes took hold, there swelled
A sense of falling, like an arrow-shower
Sent out of sight, somewhere becoming rain.

PHILIP LARKIN

Weddings

Those weddings in wartime! The deceiving comfort!
The dishonesty of words about living.
Sonorous snowy roads.
In the wind's wicked teeth I hurry down them
to a hasty wedding at the next village.
With worn-out tread and hair down in my eyes
I go inside, I famous for my dancing,
into the noisy house.
In there tensed up with nerves and with emotion
among a crowd of friends and family,

called up, distraught, the bridegroom
sitting beside his Vera, his bride.
Will in a few days put his greatcoat on
and set out coated for the war.
Will see new country, carry a rifle.
May also drop if he is hit.
His glass is fizzing but he can't drink it.
The first night may the last night.
And sadly eyeing me and bitter-minded
he leans in his despair across the table
and says, "Come on then, dance."
Drinks are forgotten. Everyone looks round.
Out I twirl to begin. Clap of my feet.
Shake.
      Scrape the floor with my toe-cap.
Whistle. Whistle. Slap hands.
Faster, leaping ceiling-high.
Moving the posters pinned up on the walls:
HITLER KAPUT
           Her eyes streaming with tears.
Already soaked in sweat and out of breath—
"Dance!"
They cry out in despair, and I dance.

When I get home my feet are log-heavy:
some drunken people from another wedding
turn up behind me. Mother must let me go.
The scene again: I see it, and again
beside the edge of a trailing tablecloth
I squat down to dance.
          She weeping
and her friends weeping. I frightened
don't feel like dancing, but you can't not dance.

Y. YEVTUSHENKO

The Housewife

My love could come home early
And find where I should be
A flour face and two eyes
Like emptied cups of tea.

My love could come and find me
Wearing an unclean room,
With an apron all around me
And my cheek rough as a crumb.

My love could come and wind me
In his new raincoat arms
And his peaked cap blind him
To my bread-and-butter charms.

If he should come home early
O the horror I should be;
But at four o'clock the horror
In his arms would be me.

I'll make my face from bottles
At seven if he comes,
Breathing scented syllables
From red lips and pink gums

While my tongue-like spoons will echo
Round the china in the room
And a slim-waisted shadow
With an apron and slim limbs

Like a vision float before him
And pour his cup of tea.
The horror will have vanished
But what's become of me?

MICHAEL BALDWIN

With Her Lips Only

This honest wife, challenged at dusk
At the garden gate, under a moon perhaps,
In scent of honeysuckle, dared to deny
Love to an urgent lover: with her lips only,
Not with her heart. It was no assignation;
Taken aback, what could she say else?
For the children's sake, the lie was venial;
"For the children's sake," she argued with her conscience.

Yet a mortal lie must follow before dawn;
Challenged as usual in her own bed,
She protests love to an urgent husband,
Not with her heart but with her lips only;
"For the children's sake," she argues with her conscience,
"For the children"—turning suddenly cold towards them.

ROBERT GRAVES

Frankie and Johnny

Frankie and Johnny were lovers, O, how that couple could love.
Swore to be true to each other, true as the stars above.
He was her man, but he done her wrong.

Frankie she was his woman, everybody knows.
She spent one hundred dollars for a suit of Johnny's clothes.
He was her man, but he done her wrong.

Frankie and Johnny went walking, Johnny in his bran' new suit,
"O good Lawd," says Frankie, "but don't my Johnny look cute?"
He was her man, but he done her wrong.

Frankie went down to Memphis; she went on the evening train.
She paid one hundred dollars for Johnny a watch and chain.
He was her man, but he done her wrong.

Frankie went down to the corner, to buy a glass of beer;
She says to the fat bartender, "Has my lovin' man bin here?
He was my man, but he done me wrong."

"Ain't gonna tell you no story, ain't gonna tell you no lie,
I seen your man 'bout an hour ago with a girl named Alice Fry.
If he's your man, he's doin' you wrong."

Frankie went back to the hotel, she didn't go there for fun,
Under her long red kimono she toted a forty-four gun.
He was her man, but he done her wrong.

Frankie went down to the hotel, looked in the window so high,
There was her lovin' Johnny a-lovin' up Alice Fry;
He was her man, but he done her wrong.

Frankie threw back her kimono; took out the old forty-four;
Roota-toot-toot, three times she shot, right through that hotel door.
She shot her man, 'cause he done her wrong.

Johnny grabbed off his Stetson. "O good Lawd, Frankie, don't
    shoot."
But Frankie put her finger on the trigger, and the gun went
    roota-toot-toot.
He was her man, but she shot him down.

"Roll me over easy, roll me over slow,
Roll me over easy, boys, 'cause my wounds are hurtin' me so,
I was her man, but I done her wrong."

With the first shot Johnny staggered; with the second shot he fell;
When the third bullet hit him, there was a new man's face in hell.
He was her man, but he done her wrong.

Frankie heard a rumblin' away down underground.
Maybe it was Johnny where she had shot him down.
He was her man, and she done him wrong.

"Oh bring on your rubber-tired hearses, bring on your rubber-tired
    hacks,
They're takin' my Johnny to the buryin' ground but they'll never
    bring him back.
He was my man, but he done me wrong."

The judge he said to the jury, "It's plain as plain can be.
This woman shot her man, so it's murder in the second degree.
He was her man, though he done her wrong."

Now it wasn't murder in the second degree, it wasn't murder in
    the third.
Frankie simply dropped her man, like a hunter drops a bird.
He was her man, but he done her wrong.

"Oh, put me in that dungeon. Oh, put me in that cell.
Put me where the northeast wind blows from the southeast corner
    of hell.
I shot my man 'cause he done me wrong."

Frankie walked up to the scaffold, as calm as a girl could be,
She turned her eyes to heaven and said, "Good Lord, I'm comin'
    to thee.
He was my man, and I done him wrong."

ANONYMOUS

The Demon Lover

"O where have you been, my long, long love,
    This long seven years and more?"
"O I'm come to seek my former vows,
    Ye granted me before."

"O hold your tongue of your former vows,
    For they will breed sad strife;
O hold your tongue of your former vows,
    For I am become a wife."

He turned him right and round about,
    And the tear blinded his eye:
"I wad never hae trodden on Irish ground,
    If it had not been for thee.

"I might hae had a king's daughter,
    Far, far beyond the sea;
I might have had a king's daughter,
    Had it not been for love o' thee."

"If ye might have had a king's daughter,
   Yersel ye had to blame:
Ye might have had taken the king's daughter,
   For ye knew that I was nane.

"If I was to leave my husband dear,
   And my two babes also,
O what have you to take me to,
   If with you I should go?"

"I hae seven ships upon the sea—
   The eighth brought me to land—
With twenty-four bold mariners,
   And music on every hand."

She has taken up her two little babes,
   Kissed them both on the chin:
"O fair ye well, my own two babes,
   For I'll never see you again."

She set her foot upon the ship,
   No mariners could she behold;
But the sails were o' the taffetie,
   And the masts of beaten gold.

She had not sailed a league, a league,
   A league but barely three,
When dismal grew his countenance,
   And darkly grew his eye.

They had not sailed a league, a league,
   A league but barely three,
Until she espied his cloven foot,
   And she wept right bitterlie.

"O hold your tongue of your weeping," says he,
  "Of your weeping now let me be;
I will shew you how the lilies grow
  On the banks of Italy."

"O what hills are yon, yon pleasant hills,
  That the sun shines sweetly on?"
"O yon are the hills of heaven," he said,
  "Where you will never win."

"O whaten a mountain is yon," she said,
  "All so dreary wi' frost and snow?"
"O yon is the mountain of hell," he cried,
  "Where you and I will go."

He strack the tap-mast wi' his hand,
  The fore-mast wi' his knee,
And he brake that gallant ship in twain,
  And sank her in the sea.

ANONYMOUS

Light Years Apart

Fingers in the Door

Careless for an instant I closed my child's fingers in the jamb. She
Held her breath, contorted the whole of her being, foetus-wise,
    against the
Burning fact of the pain. And for a moment
I wished myself dispersed in a hundred thousand pieces
Among the dead bright stars. The child's cry broke,
She clung to me, and it crowded in to me how she and I were
Light-years from any mutual help or comfort. For her I cast seed
Into her mother's womb; cells grew and launched itself as a being:
Nothing restores her to my being, or ours, even to the mother who
    within her
Carried and quickened, bore, and sobbed at her separation, despite
    all my envy,
Nothing can restore. She, I, mother, sister, dwell dispersed among
    dead bright stars:
We are there in our hundred thousand pieces!

DAVID HOLBROOK

A Considered Reply to a Child

"I love you," you said between two mouthfuls of pudding.
But not funny; I didn't want to laugh at all.
Rolling three years' experience in a ball,
You nudged it friendlily across the table.

A stranger, almost, I was flattered—no kidding.
It's not every day I hear a thing like that;

And when I do my answer's never pat.
I'm about nine times your age, ten times less able

To say—what you said; incapable of unloading
Plonk at someone's feet, like a box of bricks,
A declaration. When I try, it sticks
Like fish-bones in my throat; my eyes tingle.

What's called "passion", you'll learn, may become "overriding".
But not in me it doesn't: I'm that smart,
I can give everything and keep my heart.
Kisses are kisses. No need for souls to mingle.

Bed's bed, what's more, and you'd say it's meant for sleeping;
And, believe me, you'd be absolutely right.
With luck you'll never lie awake all night,
Someone beside you (rather like "crying") weeping.

JONATHAN PRICE

Father to Son

I do not understand this child
Though we have lived together now
In the same house for years. I know
Nothing of him, so try to build
Up a relationship from how
He was when small. Yet have I killed

The seed I spent or sown it where
The land is his and none of mine?
We speak like strangers, there's no sign

Of understanding in the air.
This child is built to my design
Yet what he loves I cannot share.

Silence surrounds us. I would have
Him prodigal, returning to
His father's house, the home he knew,
Rather than see him make and move
His world. I would forgive him too,
Shaping from sorrow a new love.

Father and son, we both must live
On the same globe and the same land.
He speaks: I cannot understand
Myself, why anger grows from grief.
We each put out an empty hand,
Longing for something to forgive.

ELIZABETH JENNINGS

Looking On

Hearing our voices raised—
Perhaps in anger,
Or in some trivial argument
That is not anger—
She screams until we stop,
And smile, and look at her,
Poised on the sheer drop
Which opens under her.

If these, her parents, show
How the gods can fail,
Squabbling on Olympus,
How can she fail

To see that anarchy
Is what one must expect,
That to be happy
One must be circumspect?

But the reverse is true
Also, when we kiss,
Seeing herself excluded
Even from that kiss.
The gods' too gross affairs
Made myths for innocent men,
So the innocent eye stares
At love in its den.

Like a strange motley beast
Out of an old myth,
Anger and love together
Make up her own myth
Of these two who cherish,
Protect, feed, deny,
In whose arms she will flourish
Or else will die.

ANTHONY THWAITE

The Orphan

To be an orphan,
To be fated to be an orphan,
How bitter is this lot!
When my father and mother were alive
I used to ride in a carriage

With four fine horses.
    But when they both died,
    My brother and my sister-in-law
    Sent me out to be a merchant.
In the south I travelled to the "Nine Rivers"
And in the east as far as Ch'i and Lu.
At the end of the year when I came home
I dared not tell them what I had suffered—
Of the lice and vermin in my head,
Of the dust in my face and eyes.
My brother told me to get ready the dinner,
My sister-in-law told me to see after the horses.
I was always going up into the hall
And running down again to the parlour.
My tears fell like rain.
In the morning they sent me to draw water,
I didn't get back till night-fall,
My hands were all sore
And I had no shoes.
I walked the cold earth
Treading on thorns and brambles.
As I stopped to pull out the thorns,
How bitter my heart was!
My tears fell and fell
And I went on sobbing and sobbing.
In winter I have no great-coat;
Nor in summer thin clothes.
It is no pleasure to be alive.
I had rather quickly leave the earth
And go beneath the Yellow Springs.
The April winds blow
And the grass is growing green
In the third month—silkworms and mulberries,
In the sixth month—the melon harvest.
I went out with the melon-cart
And just as I was coming home

The melon-cart turned over.
The people who came to help me were few,
But the people who ate the melons were many.
"At least leave me the stalks
To take home as proof.
My brother and sister-in-law are harsh,
And will be certain to call me to account."
When I got home how they shouted and scolded!
I want to write a letter and send it
To my mother and father under the earth,
And tell them I can't go on any longer
Living with my brother and sister-in-law.

ARTHUR WALEY (Translation of an
anonymous poem of the first century
A.D. in China.)

Discord in Childhood

Outside the house an ash-tree hung its terrible whips,
And at night when the wind rose, the lash of the tree
Shrieked and slashed the wind, as a ship's
Weird rigging in a storm shrieks hideously.

Within the house two voices arose, a slender lash
Whistling she-delirious rage, and the dreadful sound
Of a male thong booming and bruising, until it had drowned
The other voice in a silence of blood, 'neath the noise of the ash.

D. H. LAWRENCE

In This City

In this city, perhaps a street.
In this street, perhaps a house.
In this house, perhaps a room
And in this room a woman sitting,
Sitting in the darkness, sitting and crying
For someone who has just gone through the door
And who has just switched off the light
Forgetting she was there.

ALAN BROWNJOHN

The Evil Eye

(from READINGS OF HISTORY)

Last night we sat with the stereopticon,
laughing at genre views of 1906,
till suddenly, gazing straight into
that fringed and tasselled parlor, where the vestal
spurns an unlikely suitor
with hairy-crested plants to right and left,
my heart sank. It was terrible.
I smelled the mildew in those swags of plush,
dust on the eyepiece bloomed to freaks of mould.
I knew beyond all doubt how dead that couple was.

Today, a fresh clean morning.
Your camera stabs me unawares,
right in my mortal part.
A womb of celluloid already
contains my dotage and my total absence.

ADRIENNE RICH

A Photograph

The cardboard shows me how it was
When the two girl cousins went paddling,
Each one holding one of my mother's hands,
And she the big girl—some twelve years or so.
All three stood still to smile through their hair
At the uncle with the camera. A sweet face,
My mother's, that was before I was born.
And the sea, which appears to have changed less,
Washed their terribly transient feet.

Some twenty—thirty—years later
She'd laugh at the snapshot. "See Betty
And Dolly," she'd say, "and look how they
Dressed us for the beach." The sea holiday
Was her past, mine is her laughter. Both wry
With the laboured ease of loss.

Now she's been dead nearly as many years
As that girl lived. And of this circumstance
There is nothing to say at all.
Its silence silences.

SHIRLEY TOULSON

For a Woman with a Fatal Illness

The verdict has been given and you lie quietly
Beyond hope, hate, revenge, even self-pity.

You accept gratefully the gifts—flowers, fruit—
Clumsily offered now that your visitors too

Know you must certainly die in a matter of months,
They are dumb now, reduced only to gestures,

Helpless before your news, perhaps hating
You because you are the cause of their unease.

I, too, watching from my temporary corner,
Feel impotent and wish for something violent—

Whether as sympathy only, I am not sure—
But something at least to break the terrible tension.

Death has no right to come so quietly.

ELIZABETH JENNINGS

The Effort of Love

I am worn out
with the effort of trying to love people
and not succeeding.

Now I've made up my mind
I love nobody, I'm going to love nobody,
I'm not going to tell any lies about it
and it's final.

If there's a man here and there, or a woman
whom I can really like,
that's quite enough for me.

And if by a miracle a woman happened to come along
who warmed the cockles of my heart
I'd rejoice over the woman and the warmed cockles of my heart
so long as it didn't all fizzle out in talk.

D. H. LAWRENCE

SECTION 10
Laughs and Afterthoughts

The Irish Pig

'Twas an evening in November,
As I very well remember,
I was strolling down the street in drunken pride,
But my knees were all a'flutter
So I landed in the gutter,
And a pig came up and lay down by my side.

Yes, I lay there in the gutter
Thinking thoughts I could not utter,
When a colleen passing by did softly say,
"Ye can tell a man that boozes
By the company he chooses."—
At that, the pig got up and walked away!

ANONYMOUS

Limericks

MANNERS

There was a young lady of Tottenham,
Who'd no manners, or else she'd forgotten 'em;
 At tea at the vicar's
 She tore off her knickers
Because, she explained, she felt 'ot in 'em.

DO NOT SPIT

There was an old man of Darjeeling
Who travelled from London to Ealing
    It said on the door,
      "Please don't spit on the floor,"
So he carefully spat on the ceiling.

THE LOST WEEKEND

There was a young lady from Joppa
Who came a Society cropper.
    She went to Ostend
    With a gentleman friend
And the rest of the story's improper.

THE LATE LAMENTED

A novice was driving a car,
When, down Porlock, his son said, "Papa,
    If you drive at this rate
    We are bound to be late—
Drive faster!"—He did, and they are.

ANONYMOUS

Epitaphs

FROM ABERDEEN

Here lies the bones of Elizabeth Charlotte
Born a virgin, died a harlot
She was aye a virgin at seventeen
A remarkable thing in Aberdeen.

A TOMBSTONE IN SUTTON

Here lies my poor wife,
    Without bed or blankit,
But dead as a door-nail,
    God be thankit.

MARY ANN

Mary Ann has gone to rest,
Safe at last on Abraham's breast,
Which may be nuts for Mary Ann
But it's certainly rough on Abraham.

A DENTIST

Stranger! Approach this spot with gravity!
John Brown is filling his last cavity.

A CHILD OF SEVEN MONTHS

If I am so quickly done for
What on earth was I begun for?

PASSPORT TO PARADISE

He passed the bobby without any fuss,
And he passed the cart of hay,
He tried to pass a swerving bus,
And then he passed away.

MANNA FROM HEAVEN, NOT ANNA

The children of Israel wanted bread
The Lord he sent them manna
But this good man he wanted a wife
And the Devil sent him Anna.

THE ARTFUL DODGER

Here lies Bill Dodge
Who dodged all good
And dodged a deal of evil
But after dodging all he could
He could not dodge the Devil.

ANONYMOUS

FOR HIS WIFE

Here lies my wife.
Here let her lie!
Now she's at rest
And so am I.

JOHN DRYDEN

FOR HIMSELF

Here lies Marc Connelly.
　　Who?

　　　　　MARC CONNELLY
　　　　　(Author of "Green Pastures")

Uncultivated Accent

The Dago, the Injun, the Chink, the Jew,
The Darkie, the Parsee pale,
They spik-a de Eengleesh unlike you—
O Pedigree-parasite, Thoroughbred's-tail,
With accent pickled in Oxford ale—
But the faces and races "beyond the pale",
Are *they* so funny—or *you*?

　　　　　　　INCOGNITO

Hunter Trials

It's awf'lly bad luck on Diana,
　Her ponies have swallowed their bits;
She fished down their throats with a spanner
　And frightened them all into fits.

So now she's attempting to borrow.
　Do lend her some bits, Mummy, *do*;
I'll lend her my own for tomorrow,
　But to-day I'll be wanting them too.

Just look at Prunella on Guzzle,
    The wizardest pony on earth;
Why doesn't she slacken his muzzle
    And tighten the breech in his girth?

I say, Mummy, there's Mrs. Geyser
    And doesn't she look pretty sick?
I bet it's because Mona Lisa
    Was hit on the hock with a brick.

Miss Blewett says Monica threw it,
    But Monica says it was Joan,
And Joan's very thick with Miss Blewitt,
    So Monica's sulking alone.

And Margaret failed in her paces,
    Her withers got tied in a noose,
So her coronets caught in the traces
    And now all her fetlocks are loose.

Oh, it's me now. I'm terribly nervous.
    I wonder if Smudges will shy.
She's practically certain to swerve as
    Her Pelham is over one eye.

.   .   .   .   .   .

Oh wasn't it naughty of Smudges?
    Oh, Mummy, I'm sick with disgust.
She threw me in front of the Judges,
    And my silly old collarbone's bust.

JOHN BETJEMAN

Diversions

MANNERS

I eat my peas with honey
I've done it all my life
It makes the peas taste funny
But it keeps 'em on the knife!

ANONYMOUS

TOMATO-JUICE

An accident happened to my brother Jim
When somebody threw a tomato at him—
Tomatoes are juicy and don't hurt the skin,
But this one was specially packed in a tin.

ANONYMOUS

WHOLLY MATRIMONY

He was rich and old and she
Was thirty-two or thirty-three.
She gave him fifteen years to live—
The only thing she meant to give.

JUSTIN RICHARDSON

ULTRA-MODERN NURSERY RHYME

Hush-a-bye, baby, your milk's in the tin,
Mummy has got you a nice sitter-in;
Hush-a-bye, baby, now don't get a twinge
While Mummy and Daddy are out on the binge.

ANONYMOUS

FAULTS, MALE AND FEMALE

Men they may have many faults
But women only two—
Everything they say
And everything they do.

ANONYMOUS

WINE, WOMEN AND WEDDING

The glances over cocktails
That seemed to be so sweet
Don't seem quite so amorous
Over the Shredded Wheat.

ANONYMOUS

The President's Visit

The President visited us today,
his face a beaming china chamber-pot.
The male nurses had changed the sheets before
he came. The floor was swept of bandages
that had collected there with bits of skin—
what with the casualties piling in hard
even the sweepers have been asked to help
the surgeons. Anyway, the President
came, smiling, of course, and walked down the row
of beds. He walked slowly, naturally,
and his words foamed at his mouth like lather
collected round a leak in a drain-pipe.
He took hours reaching my bed and paused

frequently by others, raising a hand
like a dog raises his leg by a lamp-post,
a sort of blessing, you see, bestowed
on the bleeding soldiers. I must say though,
between you and me, mind, he looked something
like a bull with his snout of a mouth
as he wandered among the gored matadors
of his Republic's army. I wanted
to talk to him but he was such a haystack
of a loaded camel through the needle-eye
of this ward, so ponderously weighed
by the burden of his official visit,
that I thought a donkey can't be as slow,
and I was dangling the carrot of my
broken arm at him, too, not being able
to wave. Hell, I thought, the others have just
wounds, maybe one or two with fractured skulls
and one shot in a place I'm sure
the President wouldn't be shown—then
an awful thing happened. My weak bladder
is no secret, and as he approached me
it grew worse. Damn it, I thought, if he raises
his hand at me and I think of that dog
again, this bed will turn to a lamp-post.
This thought just about deflated
the bloated opulence of his visit
which had glowed so benignly in this ward
like a setting sun. My lavatory—
attendant's mind is my own undoing
at times, I was thinking when he reached
my bed. And what was I supposed to do then?
Hold his porcelain ears like the handles
of a chamber-pot and piss in his face?
It isn't easy with a broken arm.

ZULFIKAR GHOSE

In the Cemetery

"You see those mothers squabbling there?"
Remarks the man of the cemetery.
"One says in tears, ' 'Tis mine lies here!'
Another, 'Nay, mine, you Pharisee!'
Another, 'How dare you move my flowers
And put your own on this grave of ours!'
But all their children were laid therein
At different times, like sprats in a tin.

"And then the main drain had to cross,
And we moved the lot some nights ago,
And packed them away in the general foss
With hundreds more. But their folks don't know,
And as well cry over a new-laid drain
As anything else, to ease your pain!"

THOMAS HARDY

Song of the Battery Hen

We can't grumble about accommodation:
we have a new concrete floor that's
always dry, four walls that are
painted white, and a sheet-iron roof
the rain drums on. A fan blows warm air
beneath our feet to disperse the smell
of chicken-shit and, on dull days,
fluorescent lighting sees us.

You can tell me: if you come by
the North Door, I am in the twelfth pen
on the left-hand side of the third row
from the floor; and in that pen
I am usually the middle one of three.
But even without directions, you'd
discover me. I have the same orange-
red comb, yellow beak and auburn
feathers; but as the door opens and you
hear above the electric-fan a kind of
one-word wail, I am the one
who sounds loudest in my head.

Listen. Outside this house there's an
orchard with small moss-green apple
trees; beyond that, two fields of
cabbages; then, on the far side of
the road, a broiler-house. Listen:
one cockerel grows out of there, as
tall and proud as the first hour of sun.
Sometimes I stop calling with the others
to listen, and wonder if he hears me.

The next time you come here, look for me.
Notice the way I sound inside my head.
God made us all quite differently,
and blessed us with this expensive home.

EDWIN BROCK

A Way of Looking at Things

My son can see a man's face
In the remains of the chicken!
Figures appear on the walls
And (strange this), there are
Cities in the fire.
Last night I saw him looking
At me. No laughter on his face.
No words spoken. Just a long
Thoughtful look which I
Pretended not to notice.

JIM BURNS

Index to Poets